CATHERINE
OF SIENA

CATHERINE OF SIENA

Giuliana Cavallini OP

continuum
LONDON • NEW YORK

Continuum
The Tower Building, 11 York Road, London SE1 7NX
15 East 26th Street, New York NY 10010

www.continuumbooks.com

First published 1998
This edition first published 2005

British Library Cataloguing-in-Publication Data
A catalogue record for this book is available from the British Library.

ISBN 0 8264 7662 7

Typeset by Keystroke, Jacaranda Lodge, Wolverhampton
Printed and bound in Great Britain by Biddles Ltd, www.biddles.co.uk

Contents

To the blessed memory of Pope Paul VI
who acknowledged Catherine
as Doctor of the Church

Editorial foreword

St Anselm of Canterbury (1033–1109) once described himself as someone with faith seeking understanding. In words addressed to God he says 'I long to understand in some degree thy truth, which my heart believes and loves. For I do not seek to understand that I may believe, but I believe in order to understand.'

This is what Christians have always inevitably said, either explicitly or implicitly. Christianity rests on faith, but it also has content. It teaches and proclaims a distinctive and challenging view of reality. It naturally encourages reflection. It is something to think about; something about which one might even have second thoughts.

But what have the greatest Christian thinkers said? And is it worth saying? Does it engage with modern problems? Does it provide us with a vision to live by? Does it make sense? Can it be preached? Is it believable?

The *Outstanding Christian Thinkers* series is offered to readers with questions like these in mind. It aims to provide clear, authoritative and critical accounts of outstanding Christian writers from New Testament times to the present. It ranges across the full spectrum of Christian thought to include Catholic and Protestant thinkers, thinkers from East and West, thinkers ancient, mediaeval and modern.

The series draws on the best scholarship currently available, so it will interest all with a professional concern for the history of Christian ideas. But contributors also write for general readers who have little or no previous knowledge of the subjects to be dealt with. Its volumes should therefore prove helpful at a popular as well as an academic level. For the most part they are devoted to a single thinker, but occasionally the subject is a movement or school of thought.

The subject of the present volume, St Catherine of Siena (Caterina di Giacomo di Benincasa) is one of the three women Doctors of the Roman Catholic Church. Best known for her *Dialogue of Divine Providence* and a collection of over 300 letters

(Catherine was one of the great correspondents of her age), she is a major figure in the history of Christian literature. Her writings, especially her letters, suggest that she was a formidably independent individual with a strongly practical nature. They also offer a consistently presented theological vision which is at once simple (in that it can be stated fairly quickly) and orthodox (in that it brings together the essentials of Christian doctrine). Those who read them carefully will find in them the work of someone of immense sensitivity and insight when it comes to reflecting on the meaning and significance of the Christian gospel.

Experts on St Catherine need no introduction to the author of this book. Long associated with the study of Catherine, Professor Giuliana Cavallini is responsible for providing twentieth-century readers with the standard critical edition of the text of Catherine's *Dialogue*. In this book, however, she offers an account of St Catherine's teaching with an eye on everyone, not just the experts. Her aim is straightforwardly to explain what Catherine wrote, how her writings arose from her own experience, and what she has to say to people today. Prospective readers of what follows can therefore look forward to learning what an expert has to say about an expert among the ranks of outstanding Christian thinkers.

Brian Davies OP

Preface

St Catherine of Siena (1347–80)
Patroness of Europe

by Timothy Radcliffe OP

Catherine's Europe was, like our world today, marked by violence and an uncertain future: the papacy had fled to Avignon, splitting the Church and dividing countries, cities and religious orders, including our own; cities were being decimated by the bubonic plague, known as the Black Death; there was a decline of vitality in the Church, a loss of a sense of purpose and a crisis of religious life.

Catherine refused to resign herself in the face of this suffering and division. In the words of Pope John Paul II, she dived 'into the thick of the ecclesiastical and social issues of her time'.[1] She addressed political and religious rulers, either in person or through letters, and clearly told them their faults and their Christian duty. She did not hesitate even to tell the Pope that he must be brave and go back to Rome. She went to the prisons and cared for the poor and the sick. She was consumed by an urgency to bring God's love and mercy to everyone.

Above all, Catherine struggled for peace. She was convinced that 'not by the sword or by war or by violence' could good be achieved, but 'through peace and through constant humble prayer'.[2] Yet she never sacrificed truth or justice for a cheap or easy peace. She reminded the rulers of Bologna that to seek peace without justice was like smearing ointment on a wound that needed to be cauterized.[3] She knew that to be a peacemaker was to follow the steps of Christ, who made peace between God and humanity. And thus the peacemaker must sometimes face Christ's own fate, and suffer rejection. The peacemaker is 'another Christ crucified'. Our own world is also torn by violence: ethnic and tribal violence in Africa and the Balkans; the threat of nuclear war; violence in our cities and families. Catherine invites us to have the courage to be peacemakers, even if this means that we must suffer persecution and rejection ourselves.

Peace, for Catherine, meant, above all, peace in the Church, the healing of the Great Schism. Here we see both her intense love of the Church, which for her was 'no other than Christ himself',[4] and her courage and freedom. She so loved the Church that she did not hesitate to denounce the failings of the clergy and bishops in their pursuit of wealth and position, and called for the Church to be the mystery of Christ in the world, the humble servant of all. She even dared to tell God what to do, when she prayed:

> You know how and you are able and it is your will, so I plead with you to have mercy on the world, and to restore the warmth of charity and peace and unity to holy Church. It is my will that you do not delay any longer.[5]

The Church in our time also suffers from divisions, caused by mis-understanding, intolerance and a loss of 'the warmth of charity and peace'. Today the love of the Church is often assumed to mean an uncritical silence. One must not 'rock the boat'! But Catherine could never be silent. She wrote to some cardinals, 'Be silent no longer. Cry out with a hundred thousands voices. I see that the world is destroyed through silence. Christ's spouse is pallid, her colour has been drained from her.'[6] May St Catherine teach us her deep love of the Body of Christ, and the wisdom and courage to speak truthfully and openly with words that unite rather than divide, which illuminate rather than obscure, and which heal rather than wound.

Catherine's relationships with her friends, and especially her Dominican brothers and sisters, was marked by the same combin-ation of love and boldness of speech ('parrhesia', e.g. Acts 4:31, 2 Cor 7:4). She regarded each friend as a gift from God, to be loved 'very closely, with a particular love'.[7] She believed that their mutual friendship was an opportunity 'to bring each other to birth in the gentle presence of God',[8] and a proclamation of 'the glory and praise of God's name to others'. But this love did not prevent her from speaking very frankly to her friends, and telling her brethren exactly what they should do, including her beloved Raymond of Capua, who became Master of the Order in the year of her death. There can be no love without truth, nor truth without love. This is how she prayed for her friends:

Eternal God,
I pray to you
for all those you have given me
to love with a special love
and with special concern.
Let them be illuminated with your light.
Let all imperfection be taken from them,
so that in truth
they may work in your garden,
where you have assigned them.[9]

If the Dominican Family is to become, in Catherine's words, 'a very spacious, gladsome and fragrant, a most delightful garden',[10] then we must learn both her capacity for mutual friendship and for truthfulness. Our friendship as men and women, religious and lay people, is a great gift for the Order and for the Church, but it often is marred by wounds of which we hardly dare to speak. If we are to work together as preachers of the gospel, then we must speak to each other with Catherine's frankness and trust, so that 'in truth they may work in your garden'.

Catherine was a passionate woman with big desires: for union with God, for the spread of the gospel and for the good of the whole human family. Desire expands our hearts. She told God: 'you make the heart big, not stingy – so big that it has room in its loving charity for everyone'.[11] God said to Catherine, 'I who am infinite God want you to serve me with what is infinite, and you have nothing infinite except your soul's desire.'[12]

How can we grow as men and women who are touched by Catherine's passion for God? How can we be liberated from smallness of heart and contentment with little satisfactions? Perhaps it is through discovering, as did Catherine, that God is present in the very centre of our being and identity. The passion for God is not a taste to be acquired, like a love of football. It is there in the core of my being, waiting to be discovered. Our world is marked by a deep hunger for identity. For many people today the urgent question is: 'Who am I?' This was Catherine's question. The contemporary search for self-knowledge is often a narcissistic preoccupation with self, an introverted concentration on one's own well-being and fulfilment. But for Catherine, when I finally see myself as I am, I do not discover a little nugget of lonely selfhood. In what Catherine called 'the cell of self-knowledge'

I discover myself being loved into existence. She described herself as 'dwelling in the cell of self-knowledge in order to know better God's goodness towards her'.[13] If I dare to make that journey towards self-knowledge, then I shall discover how small, flawed and finite I am, but I shall also see that I am utterly loved and valued. God told Catherine: 'It was with providence that I created you, and when I contemplated my creature in myself, I fell in love with the beauty of my creation.'[14]

So Catherine offers a liberating answer to the contemporary quest for identity. It takes us far away from a false identity based on status or wealth or power. For at the heart of our being is the God whose love sustains us in being. This is the place of contemplative prayer, where one meets the God who delights in loving and forgiving, and whose own goodness we taste. Here we discover the secret of Catherine's peace and her dynamism, her confidence and her humility. This is what made this young woman, with little formal education, a great preacher. This is what gave her the freedom to speak and to listen. This is what gave her the courage to dive in and address the great issues of her time. With the help of her prayers we may do likewise.

1   Apostolic Letter, *L'Osservatore Romano*, no. 40 (1611),
     English edition.
2   D. 15.
3   L. 268.
4   L. 171.
5   O. 24.
6   L. 16.
7   D. 41.
8   L. 292.
9   O. 21.
10 D. 158.
11 O. 21.
12 D. 92.
13 D. 1.
14 D. 135.

Note: This was originally published as a letter to the Dominican Order in April 2000 to celebrate the naming of St Catherine of Siena as one of the Patrons of Europe.

The writings of Catherine of Siena

The writings of Catherine of Siena that we have include:

The Letters. They cover a period of about ten years (1370–80). The addressees belong to almost all social stations, from the two Popes of Catherine's public activity, kings and queens, to humble artisans or the members of her own family. They number 381.

The Dialogue: an exchange of questions and answers between Catherine and God the Father about the most important problems of humankind. Catherine dictated it at intervals, between the autumn of 1377 and October 1378.

The Prayers were not dictated by Catherine but as she used to pray aloud her disciples thought of writing down what she was saying. Most of those that they recorded belong to the Roman period of Catherine's life, from December 1378 to the spring of 1380.

Manuscript collections of Catherine of Siena's works are kept in several libraries, in England (Oxford, Cambridge, London) as well as in Italy and elsewhere.

A few years after the introduction of the art of printing in Italy, when almost exclusive preference was given to the Bible and to great classics, Azzoguidi issued the first printed edition of the *Dialogue* (Bologna, 1472/75). Catherine's 'book' had already been translated into Latin, which, at that time, could be read by learned people all over Europe: the first printed Latin edition was given by Bernardino de Misintis (Brixiae, 1496). But English was the first modern language into which the *Dialogue* was translated, in the early fifteenth century, for the Bridgettine nuns of Syon Abbey. Wynkyn de Worde printed it in 1519 under the title of *The Orcherd of Syon*. Editions of the *Dialogue* in Italian, Latin and other languages from 1472 to the present day amount to about seventy, which makes an average of one edition every seven or eight years, besides ten abridged editions in various languages.

A small collection of 31 Letters was printed by Fontanesi (Bologna, 1492), soon to be followed by a beautiful volume containing 353 letters collected and printed by Aldo Manuzio (Venice, 1500), who included in the same volume 26 *Prayers*. At the beginning of the eighteenth century, Girolamo Gigli edited the complete works of Catherine of Siena, including her biography by Raymond of Capua, his aim being to demonstrate that Catherine's Sienese language was just as good as, or maybe better than, the more generally appreciated language of Florence. Recent editions include 381 letters. A critical edition, the first volume of which (88 letters) appeared in 1940, is still to be completed.

Further reading

Gabriella Anodal, *Il linguaggio cateriniano: indice delle immagini* (Siena, 1983).

Atti del Congresso Internazionale di Studi Cateriniani, Siena–Roma, 24–29 aprile 1980 (Rome, 1981).

Atti del Simposio Internazionale Cateriniano-Bernardiniano, Siena, 17–20 Aprile 1980 (Siena, 1982).

Anna Maria Balducci, *Massime di reggimento civile di Santa Caterina da Siena* (Rome, 1947; repr. 1971).

Lidia Bianchi and Diega Giunta, *Iconografia di S. Caterina da Siena – L'lmmagine* (Rome, 1988)

Catherine of Siena, *La città prestata: consigli ai politici*, ed. Gianfranco Morra (Rome, 1990).

Catherine of Siena, *Il Dialogo: Dialogo della Divina Provvidenza ovvero Libro della Divina Dottrina*, ed. Giuliana Cavallini (Rome, 1968; 2nd edn, Siena, 1995).

Catherine of Siena, *The Dialogue*, trans. Suzanne Noffke (London and New York, 1980).

Catherine of Siena, *Epistolario di santa Caterina da Siena*, ed. Eugenio Duprè Theseider (Rome, 1940–).

Catherine of Siena, *The Letters of St Catherine of Siena*, trans. Suzanne Noffke (Binghamton, NY, 1988).

Catherine of Siena, *Il Messaggio di Santa Caterina da Siena: dottore della Chiesa; tutto il pensiero della vergine senese esposto con le sue parole in forma moderna*, ed. P. Carlo Riccardi (Rome, 1988).

Catherine of Siena, *Le Orazioni*, ed. Giuliana Cavallini (Italian and Latin texts on facing pages; Rome, 1978; 2nd edn, without Latin text, Siena, 1993).

Catherine of Siena, *La Verità dell'Amore*, selected writings with extensive introduction by G. Cavallini (Rome, 1978).

Catherine of Siena, *The Prayers of Catherine of Siena*, trans. Suzanne Noffke (New York, 1983).

Mary Ann Fatula, *Catherine of Siena's Way* (rev. edn; Collegeville, MN, 1990).

Kenelm Foster and Mary John Ronayne (trans. and ed.), *I, Catherine: Selected Writings of St Catherine of Siena* (London, 1980).

Suzanne Noffke, *Catherine of Siena: Vision Through a Distant Eye* (A Michael Glazier Book; Collegeville, MN, 1996) (contains a large bibliography of works on Catherine of Siena in English).

Piero Pajardi, *Caterina: la santa della politica: ricerche e riflessioni sul pensiero etico, giuridico, sociale e politico di Santa Caterina da Siena* (Milan, 1993).

Giorgio Papàsogli, *Sangue e fuoco: Caterina da Siena* (3rd edn; Rome, 1989).

Raymond of Capua, *The Life of Catherine of Siena*, trans. Conleth Kearns (Wilmington, DE, 1980).

Carlo Riccardi, *Caterina da Siena e l'Eucaristia: saggio* (Siena, 1995).

Carlo Riccardi, *Maria Santissima nella vita e nel pensiero di S. Caterina da Siena: saggio* (Siena, 1996).

Carlo Riccardi, *Il pensiero filosofico e mistico di S. Caterina da Siena: saggio* (Siena, 1994).

Vincenzo Romano OP, 'Il Mistero di Maria in S. Caterina da Siena', *Eco di S. Domenico*, LXIV, no. 4 (1996).

Lina Zanini and M. Carlotta Paterna, *Bibliografia Analitica di S. Caterina da Siena: 1901–1950* (Rome, 1971), 1951–1975 (Rome, 1985), 1976–1985 (Rome, 1989).

Abbreviations

D   *Dialogue*; followed by Roman numeral of the section including the quotation.
      S. Caterina da Siena, IlDialogo, ed. G. Cavallini (Rome, 1968; Siena, 1995).

L   *Letters*; followed by Arabic numeral of the letter quoted according to Tommaseo's numbering, normally used in Italian editions.
      Lettere di S. Caterina da Siena, ed. L. Ferretti (5 vols; Siena, 1918–30). The texts quoted have been occasionally checked with E. Duprè-Theseider's critical edition (Rome, 1940), which includes only 88 letters.

P   *Prayers*; followed by Roman numeral of the prayer including the passage quoted in the numbering of the critical edition.
      S. Caterina da Siena, Le Orazioni, ed. G. Cavallini (Rome, 1978).

Life by Raymond of Capua, with Arabic numeral of the paragraph including the passage quoted.
      B. Raimondo da Capua, Vita di S. Caterina da Siena, Ital. trans. from Latin G. Tinagli, ed. G. D'Urso (Sth edn; Siena, 1982).

All the translations from St Catherine's writings and biography are mine; this is why reference is given to Italian texts.

Chronology

(Note: Some of the dates referring to events in Catherine's life are conjectural, since her early biographers apparently did not think these were important.)

1305 5 June. Clement V (Bertrand de Got) is elected Pope, the first to reside in France.

1337 The beginning of the Hundred Years War.

1343 Cola di Rienzi is sent to Avignon to ask Pope Clement VI to come to Rome.

1347 Four years later Rienzi assumes power in the city: his ambition is to revive the glories of ancient times.

25 March. Catherine and her twin sister are born in Siena, raising to 24 the number of the children of Iacopo di Benincasa and Lapa de' Piagenti.

1348 The Black Death ravages Europe reducing its population to about two-thirds.

Lapa gives birth to her 25th and last child.

1353 Joanna of Anjou, Queen of Naples, sells the city of Avignon to the papacy. King John II of France refuses peace offered by Edward III of England in exchange for sovereignty over Gascony, Normandy and Ponthieu.

On her way home from the house of a married sister, Catherine is shown a beautiful vision: the Lord Jesus, clad in pontifical vestments, is sitting on a throne; near him are the apostles Peter, Paul and John. The Lord smiles at the little girl and blesses her with the sign of the cross. Thus begins Catherine's love story. The vision has given her a precocious maturity, and her only concern is how to please her beloved. In an effort to imitate the Desert Fathers she seeks prayerful solitude in a small cave just outside the city walls. Growing darkness makes her realize that her family must be anxious and she hastens back home.

1354   After a few years' absence, Cola di Rienzi returns triumphantly to Rome with the title of Senator, but is soon killed in a riot.

Having been enlightened on the beauty of serving God in perfect purity of body and mind, Catherine makes a vow of perpetual virginity. Though only seven, she is fully aware of what that commitment means.

1356   A Turkish army captures Gallipoli to use as an operational base for the conquest of the Balkans. Victory of the Black Prince at Poitiers; King John of France and the dauphin are taken as prisoners to England.

1357   Representatives of the Italian Papal States gather at Fano and approve Cardinal Albornoz's *Constitutiones Aegidianae*, an important body of statutes giving uniform regulations to the Papal States without disregarding local situations and needs.

1359

Catherine is now twelve and Lapa dreams of a good match for her. She insists that the girl should pay more attention to making herself attractive; Bonaventura, one of her older daughters, is her ally. Yielding to their joint pressure,

Catherine consents to wear finer clothes and be more careful of her hair.

1360 The peace of Brétigny marks a pause in the Hundred Years War.

1362

August. Bonaventura dies in childbirth. Catherine interprets the event as a warning and a punishment for her own yielding to vanity.

To show that she is still determined to keep her vow, on the advice of Fr Thomas della Fonte, her first spiritual confidant and director, she cuts her hair short. Lapa is furious; she imposes all the household work on the rebel and deprives her of the small room where she used to retire and pray. The result is not what she expected: Catherine realizes there is a 'secret cell' within us, where at any moment, whatever one may be engaged in, God's presence can be found. One day she summons the whole family and declares that she is willing to be their servant to the end of her life, but will never consent to marry, having already taken the Lord Jesus Christ as her spouse. At this Iacopo tells the family that from now on nobody should dare to disturb Catherine or try to dissuade her from the way of life she has chosen, since her choice is not a childish whim, but a response to a call from on high.

1363 Muslim advance in Eastern Europe.

Catherine joins the Sisters of Penance of St Dominic and is clothed in the white tunic and

black cloak which members of
that lay branch of the Order of
Preachers used to wear in the
fourteenth century even though
living with their own families. For
the following four years, she leads
a life of prayer and penance,
scarcely ever leaving her room
except to attend religious offices
at St Dominic's, and speaking only
to her confessor.

1366 Amadeus VI of Savoy comes
to the rescue of the Byzan-
tine Emperor John V and
defeats the Turks who are
besieging Constantinople.

She is taught by the Lord Jesus
Christ, who often visits her cell,
while evil spirits do their best or
their worst to disturb her.

1367 Pope Urban V makes an
effort to bring the Holy See
back to Rome; on 30 April
1367 he leaves Avignon,
lands at Corneto on 3 June,
and enters Rome on
16 October. Meanwhile
(22 August) Cardinal
Albornoz has died.

Instead of entering her room, the
Lord Jesus stays at the threshold
and asks Catherine to come out
and take part in the life of her
family and her city. Thus begins a
period of intense activity, which
does not, however, hinder Catherine's intimacy with God. She first
devotes herself to nursing the sick
in the various city hospitals, then
her help is sought to obtain the
conversion of notorious sinners or
to restore peace between warring
families or individuals. A group of
followers begins to gather around
Catherine including men and
women, members of religious
orders and lay people of various
social levels. Catherine is just out
of her teens and most of them are
older than she is, but they understand that she is giving them a
new kind of life and call her
'mamma'.

1370 Perugia rebels against the
French papal legate.

As the fame of Catherine's outstanding spiritual gifts begins to

Urban V leaves Rome (17 April) for Viterbo and announces his intention of returning to Avignon. He sails from Corneto in September, lands in France in November and about one month later (10 December) he dies, as St Bridget of Sweden had warned him. On 30 December Pierre Roger de Beaufort succeeds him as Gregory XI.

spread beyond Siena, people from abroad seek her advice and she replies by letters which she dictates to her friends, since she has not learnt to write.

1371 The new Pope's policy to check the power of the Visconti, the lords of Milan, finds supporters in northern Italy, in the Queen of Naples and King Louis I of Hungary; Tuscan city-states take a stand against it.

1372 Gregory announces to the consistory his intention to move to Rome.
The English fleet is defeated at La Rochelle.
St Bridget of Sweden dies in Rome.

1373

Probable date of Catherine's letter to Bernabò Visconti, insisting on loyalty to the Church.

1374 17 April. Gregory XI renews his declaration to the consistory of his intention to leave for Rome.

The English possessions in France are now reduced to Calais, Bordeaux and Bayonne.

Alfonso di Valdaterra, St Bridget's former director, is sent to Catherine by Gregory to seek her prayers for himself and the Church. In May Catherine is in Florence, gaining new friends and disciples. She is given Raymond of Capua as director, which she considers a very special gift of the Blessed Virgin. Back in Siena,

Catherine spends the whole summer in nursing and assisting the plague-stricken, as a severe recurrence of the Black Death is claiming many victims in the city, including some of Catherine's relatives. In the autumn she visits the Dominican monastery at Montepulciano and venerates the incorrupt body of Blessed Agnes, its foundress.

1375 Naples, Genoa, and other Italian states offer their galleys to Gregory on the assumption that the transfer of the papal court to Rome is imminent. But the prospect that his presence may help France and England come to terms causes the Pope to linger in France. It is in fact through his good offices that the Truce of Bruges is signed.

In the spring and early summer Catherine is in Pisa and Lucca, trying to dissuade the local authorities from joining the antipapal league fostered by Bernabò Visconti, and to persuade them to join the Crusade.
On 1 April she receives the stigmata of Christ's passion in the Pisan church of St Cristina. Catherine writes to Queen Elizabeth of Hungary and warns her of the danger of the invasion of her country by the Turkish army advancing in Eastern Europe.

1376 In spite of Catherine's efforts, Pisa and Lucca join the antipapal league (12 March) and Bologna revolts (19 March). John Hawkwood's mercenary soldiers fight against the rebels and make havoc in Faenza. Gregory XI puts Florence, which is at the heart of the rebellion, under an interdict and the Florentines send ambassadors to Avignon to seek peace.

Catherine writes several letters to Gregory urging him to come to Rome, reform the Church, promote the Crusade: the three principal means to restore peace. She sends Raymond of Capua and some of her followers to Avignon to plead the cause of Florence. On 1 April Catherine has a significant vision: she sees Christians together with unbelievers enter the wound in the side of Christ and is given a cross and an olive branch to bring to both peoples. In May Catherine leaves for Avignon where she speaks to

Gregory, Raymond acting as interpreter. Her pleading for the cause of Florence fails, but she obtains a more important success in leading Gregory to an effective decision to move to Rome.

August. At the request of Duke Louis of Anjou, Catherine writes to Charles V of France asking him to put an end to the war against England and join the Crusade.

On the same day Gregory XI and the papal court leave Avignon for Marseilles, sailing to Italy on 2 October. But the boats have to battle against a great storm and not until two weeks later are they able to reach Savona, then Genoa, where they anchor. The French Cardinals try to persuade Gregory to go back to Avignon, but Catherine encourages him to go on to Rome, and on 29 October the fleet sails southward to Leghorn where Gregory is warmly welcomed on his arrival (7 November).

13 September. Catherine and her companions begin their journey towards Italy by land. On 3 October they arrive at Varazze and the next day they move on to Genoa where they make a longer stay, some of Catherine's followers having fallen ill.

On 7 December Gregory and the papal court land at Corneto where they stay until mid-January.

At the end of December Catherine is back in Siena.

1377   13 January. The papal fleet sails from Corneto to the mouth of the Tiber and upstream to Rome. On 17 January Gregory lands in front of St Paul's and is escorted to the Vatican by a crowd of happy people bearing flaming torches.

On 25 January Catherine is given leave by the Sienese authorities to establish a monastery in the Belcaro stronghold which Nanni di Ser Vanni, a convert of hers, has put at her disposal. About one month later the monastery of Our Lady of the Angels has its solemn inauguration: William Flete, Catherine's English Augustinian

In February Breton soldiers led by Cardinal Robert of Geneva massacre the rebellious population of Cesena.

disciple, celebrates the Eucharist in the new chapel. Catherine spends the late summer and autumn at Rocca d'Orcia as peacemaker between two rival branches of the powerful Salimbeni family and restoring the inhabitants of the Val d'Orcia to the civilized ways of living they had forgotten because of the violence and hatred of their lords. During her stay at Rocca d'Orcia, Catherine is granted that 'abundant light of truth' which will form the subject of her 'book', the *Dialogue*. For the moment she gives a summary account of it to Raymond in a long letter in her own hand, having at last learnt how to use a pen.

1378 27 March. Gregory XI dies. 8 April. Bartolomeo Prignano, Archbishop of Bari, is elected Pope. He takes the name of Urban VI, which proclaims his intention of staying in Rome. He immediately begins the task of purifying the Church from corruption and abuse; but his excessively harsh ways make him many enemies. 20 September. The cardinals, French for the most part, meet at Fondi and hold a new election: their choice is Cardinal Robert of Geneva and he takes the name of Clement VII, an ironic name for the author of the slaughter at Cesena. Thus begins the Great Schism which for about forty years will split

Wishing to put an end to the Florentine strife, Gregory XI sends Catherine to Florence as a mediator. She barely escapes being killed in a riot, but at last a treaty of peace is signed (28 July). Back in Siena in the late summer Catherine becomes engrossed in the composition of the *Dialogue*, which she has begun to dictate in the previous months and will complete within the first half of October. 28 November. In response to an order of Urban VI Catherine arrives in Rome. The next day she speaks to the Pope and the cardinals who support him, encouraging them to trust in divine Providence. In mid-December Raymond of Capua sails from the Roman seaport of Ostia to France, having been appointed papal legate to King Charles V.

Western Christianity into two and eventually three factions.

1379 From Avignon, where he has moved with his court, Clement sends Breton soldiers to Italy to fight against Urban's followers. Some of them are based in Castel Sant'Angelo – the mausoleum of Emperor Hadrian which is now the Vatican's stronghold – and are a permanent disturbance and threat to the city of Rome. On 29 April, in a decisive battle at Marino – some fourteen miles south of Rome – the army of the antipope is defeated by the Italian Company of St George, and the garrison at Castel Sant'Angelo surrenders. Christian Europe is now divided into two factions: central Italy, Venice, Milan, Genoa, Flanders and England stay with Urban VI; Savoy, Naples, Spain, Avignon, Scotland and France follow Clement VII.

Catherine spends the whole year in Rome, devoting herself to the support of the lawful Pope. She writes many letters to this end and sends Neri di Landoccio to Naples hoping he may be of help in inducing Queen Joanna to support Urban. Her yearning for the unity of the Church is like a fire consuming her young life. While she explains to both ecclesiastical and civil authorities why Urban's election must be considered lawful, her prayers to God for unity and peace in the Church are uninterrupted.

1380 At the end of January Catherine suffers what seems to have been a severe heart attack: the pain in her chest is so strong she can hardly bear it. For two days she is utterly unable to move or speak, so that her followers begin to doubt whether she is alive, but she is fully aware of what is going on, while her mind is intensely united to God. On 2 February the crisis is over, but Catherine is exhausted, although her desire to obey the Lord helps her to walk every morning to St Peter's and spend the whole day there, praying and fasting. One day she senses that the 'mystical boat' of the Church is being imposed on her shoulders and she fails under its weight. From now on she is unable to leave her bed. On 29 April at noon she dies, the Lord's last words on her lips: 'Father, into your hands I commit my soul and spirit'. Two days later, at night, her body is taken to the Dominican church of S. Maria sopra Minerva, only a few steps from the house where she died, and on the following day people flood in for a last farewell; many sick people recover. Then Catherine's body is buried in the same church.

Those who had been acquainted with Catherine had no doubt about her holiness, but her canonization was delayed because of the schism which had occurred after Gregory XI's return to Rome, the return which Catherine had ardently sought and promoted.

With the Council of Constance (1414–18) and the election of Martin V (Oddone Colonna) as Pope (1417), the unity of the Church was practically restored and the chief obstacle to her canonization was removed. On 29 June 1461, Pius II acknowledged Catherine of Siena as a saint.

In later years Catherine was named co-patron of Rome with the apostles Peter and Paul (1866) and of Italy with Francis of Assisi (1939); and recently Catherine joined Benedict, Cyril and Methodius as patron saints of Europe.

Catherine of Siena is the earliest woman ever to have earned the title of Doctor of the Church, which Pope Paul VI awarded to her on 4 October 1970.

1

Catherine and her writings

I was provided with writing so that
I might give vent to my heart
lest it should burst. (L, 272)

Catherine of Siena lived six centuries ago: how can we come to know her? And, does it matter at all that we know her? This book will try to answer both questions.

With reference to Catherine's life we have some biographical works by her contemporaries such as Raymond of Capua's *Legenda Maior*, Thomas of Anthony's *Libellus de Supplemento* and the *Processso Castellano*, the process for her canonization, so called because it was held in the diocese of Castello, Venice, gathering evidence given under oath by several persons who had met her during her lifetime.

Raymond, Catherine's spiritual director and disciple from 1374, is careful in quoting his sources, whether he learnt what he is relating from Catherine's mother or another person, or through his own experience of the event. Thomas, better known as Caffarini, after assisting Raymond in the composition of the *Legenda*, gathered the material he had not used into his *Libellus*, and included in it the notebooks of Thomas della Fonte, Catherine's first adviser, of whom we have no direct knowledge. Abridged *Legendae* were produced in order to have more copies at a time when handwriting was the only means for the diffusion of literature. Caffarini was very active in this field: he had some scriptoria where copies of the *legendae* and of Catherine's own works were made, from there to be distributed all over Italy and in other countries. He believed, and we can surely agree with him, that for a full understanding of Catherine her writings afford greater interest than the events in her life. Or we might say that while biographical events are of help for the understanding of some of her writings, the writings also throw flashes of light on Catherine's character and on the roots of her activity.

Catherine was anything but a scholar. It was not customary for fourteenth-century artisan families to send their little girls to school, even supposing that such schools existed. When she grew up, Catherine wanted to learn how to read, so that she might join in the liturgical praise of the Lord, but proved rather slow in her efforts to learn the alphabet. As she felt that she was simply wasting time, she turned to the Lord and briskly told him that if he wanted her to read he should help her; if not, she would be just as happy. Her prayer over, she found she could read but was unable to spell: for her, each word was a unity, not to be broken down into single letters.

Catherine was gifted with writing some years later, when she was thirty: in a vision or dream St John the Evangelist and St Thomas Aquinas taught her how to use a pen. But by that time, towards the end of 1377, her letters had already reached Pope Gregory XI (1370–78) and Charles V of France (1364–80) as well as many other persons of high and low condition, for her followers were ready to help by writing down her messages so that, even afterwards, she found it more convenient to dictate than to write.

In 1347, when Catherine was born, Italian was a rather young language whose Latin heritage could still be sensed, but could also already boast of three great writers, besides a number of minor poets: Dante Alighieri (1265–1321) had died 25 years before, having described heaven and earth in his own passionate way, after the conception of the universe accepted in his time; Petrarch (1304–74) was still sighing for his beloved Laura or meditating on the mountains round Vaucluse; while the Black Death then approaching Europe was soon to offer Boccaccio (1313–75) the framework for his *Decameron*.

In spite of her slowness in learning the mechanics of reading and writing, Catherine was to earn quite an honourable place among the 'great' of the 'golden century' of Italian literature, where she is the first woman author ever named. Moreover, Catherine was to be the earliest woman to earn the title of Doctor of the Church.[1]

Catherine's writings are known as *Dialogue, Prayers, Letters*. The *Letters* are particularly appreciated as literary and historical documents, while the *Dialogue* is chiefly responsible for her title of Doctor of the Church. In Raymond of Capua's biography of her we are told that about two years before her death, Catherine had such an extraordinary revelation that she asked her secretaries to be ready to write what she might dictate. From a letter to Raymond during her stay at Rocca d'Orcia, a letter that can be considered as a first sketch of the *Dialogue*, we can assume that the splendid vision was granted her in the autumn of 1377, and that before long Catherine started dictating to her secretaries. But writing went on for quite some time, since in the following months Catherine was engaged in a very important mission: that of making peace between the Holy See and the Florentine Republic. Towards the end of July a messenger entered Florence, the olive branch in his hand, and Catherine went back to Siena where, according to Raymond, she attended more assiduously to the composition of her 'book', as she used to call it. In the first days of October 1378 the work was completed.

THE DIALOGUE

This singular conversation between Catherine and a mysterious voice responding to her desires in the depths of her soul is at the same time the story of mankind in its fall and redemption, and that of every single soul striving for perfection. It starts from the desire of a soul – Catherine's or anybody else's – that, having already made some progress in the ways of the spirit, is prompted by ardent longing for the honour of God and the salvation of human souls to seek further enlightenment, since love springs from knowledge and human nature, the product of divine Love, can only attain its perfection in loving. Thus the central subject of the book is proposed in its first paragraphs.

General desire for knowledge is then specified by Catherine in four petitions: for herself, for the reform of the Church, for peace in the whole troubled world, for a particular occurrence.

For herself Catherine asks that she may atone for all the evil in the world by personal penance. The answer is that what matters is not physical penance, which is perforce limited: the Infinite requires infinite desire: love. Love is certainly due to God, but since we can be of no help to him, we are offered our needy neighbours to help in his stead; it is through neighbours that we practise either virtue or vice.

Catherine's attention is then focused on discernment, the virtue most appropriate to 'the creature that holds reason', concluding the 'Doctrine on Perfection', the answer to Catherine's petition for herself.

The second and third questions are first given short answers which are fully developed further on. In this part, a close reproduction of the brief sketch in the letter to Raymond, Catherine's understanding is drawn to the gift of redemption and the increased responsibility of the redeemed creature to respond to it, as well as to the reverence due to the Bride of Christ, then badly in need of a reform to be effected not by violence, but by prayer and loving sacrifice.

The 'Doctrine on the Bridge', which follows, is the central and most important part of the book. Man's rebellion against God – a refusal of love in the refusal of obedience – opened a great chasm between heaven and earth. Having rebelled against God, man found rebellion within himself: the powers of his soul, without the link of charity, could no longer work in harmony. Besides, nature refused subjection to man and sprouted thorns and thistles for him. But God would not suffer his loving plan to be thwarted, and sent his own Son to the rescue; he, by assuming human nature in his own divine person, made himself into a bridge spanning the deep chasm, a safe way for man to return to the Father. This was a way offered by God's love, made clearly visible in the passion of the Word incarnate, and requiring a return of love. The ascent of the mystical bridge is the progress of the soul from imperfect to most perfect love. Once memory, understanding and will have been restored to natural, harmonious interaction, the soul rises from servile affection to friendly and to filial love. Perfect love makes the soul one with Christ and gives it a share in his filial obedience which gives honour to the Father by striving towards the salvation of souls. Such mission implies labour and suffering, and this is why, on her request, Catherine is instructed about the 'Doctrine on Tears'. All tears are bred in the heart, but not all are good: some are bearers of life and some of death. Givers of death are the tears of the self-centred, who never cease to complain about their own misfortunes. Tears of life are man's companions in his progress towards perfection, which is not without suffering. It also requires enlightenment, as explained in the 'Doctrine on Light' which follows. Light is of primary importance to the pilgrims on the bridge of love; it can shine more or less brightly but cannot be negative; it might be lacking, but, if present, it is necessarily positive.

Christ did not make a bridge of himself just for his contemporaries: the way to heaven must be open to mankind throughout time to come. To this end he entrusted his Bride, the Church, with his doctrine and the ministry of the sacraments. This subject is dealt with in the teaching about the 'Mystical Body of Holy Church' which is the final section of the 'Doctrine on the Bridge'.

Then Catherine's gratitude for the teaching imparted to her bursts forth in a highly inspired hymn of thanksgiving and an ardent prayer for mercy.

The next section deals with 'Divine Providence'. It is a sort of review of the story of mankind, in the perspective of God's constant care for its welfare. In creating man God provided him with a soul portraying the perfections of the Holy Trinity; after man's fall, God enabled him to keep alive the flame of hope in redemption, through the prophets, and through the events of the Old Testament. After redemption has been achieved God's eye never ceases to watch his beloved creatures and to provide events or circumstances best suited for each one's improvement, even though particular situations may prove difficult to understand and accept. Such was the case of a man sentenced to death, the particular occurrence about which Catherine had asked to be told in her fourth petition. Yes, the sentence was cruel, but God turned it into an occasion for the man to convert and earn eternal life.

The last section of the *Dialogue* is dedicated to 'Obedience', the natural counterpart to the disobedience which had marked the very beginning of the story; it includes definitive answers to Catherine's petitions. The primal disobedience is recalled under the figure of a key, the key of obedience that Adam despised, hammered out of shape with his pride and threw into a muddy pond. Then came the sweet loving Word: he drew the key out of the mud, washed it clean in his blood and hammered it back into proper shape on the anvil of his body. On returning to heaven he left the key to his Vicar, to give to each man or woman in baptism. Everybody disposes of the key of obedience and can use it either in the general or the particular way. The general way is to comply with the law of human nature as expressed in the Ten Commandments; particular obedience is the observance of the evangelical counsels, to which one may be led by special love for this virtue as fostered by the example of the obedient Word incarnate.

The discussion is here naturally focused on religious orders, where the counsels are normally practised. They are introduced under the imagery of ships. The first is presented in as few words as possible:

Look at Benedict, how orderly did he order his little ship!

In building his own ship, Francis impressed on it the features of his beloved Lady Poverty: only a few, perfect sailors can stay in it. Dominic's boat is perfectly set to give honour to God and lead souls to salvation by the light of true science; it is a delightful garden which both the perfect and the imperfect can enjoy.

The images of the ships and of the garden, often used for the Church, may be a hint as to the contribution that religious orders are expected to give to the renewal of the Bride of Christ, the more so as the captains of the second and third ships make a remarkable portrait of the Word incarnate by complementary features: Francis, whose passionate love for Christ crucified earned for him the privilege of bearing in his body the stigmata of Christ's passion, is an image of Christ's foolish love for the human creature; while Dominic, the lover of faith and giver of truth, is as faithful a likeness of eternal Wisdom revealing God's truth and giving honour to the Father by helping human souls to attain salvation. Since love of poverty and commitment to the salvation of souls are virtues most badly lacking in the clergy and in the whole world, Francis and Dominic may be understood as holding an answer to both the second and the third petition. They are, in fact, proclaimed 'pillars of the Church'.

Such appears to be the meaning of the parallel praises of Poverty and of Obedience: both are said to be queens whose subjects enjoy peace and prosperity, having no fear of war because their wealth consists of virtues and is not such as can raise greed and strife. Having mastered their disorderly tendencies, they enjoy perfect freedom. They are warmed by the sun of divine grace which makes their soil richly fruitful.

As regards Benedict's vessel, a pattern of perfect order, it might be taken as an image of the Church sailing on the stormy sea of earthly history with no security but the promise of the Lord, 'I am with you to the end of time' (Matt 28:20).

As the *Dialogue* nears its end, obedience is said to be God's favourite virtue, the one most especially appealing to his kindness. The choice of the miracles of obedience here related is no doubt intentional: their having operated on the four elements then supposed to be constitutive of the universe is certainly meant to imply that nature's rebellion to man as a consequence of sin can be overcome when friendship between God and man is restored by obedience: 'everything obeys the obedient'.

The last words to Catherine are of praise to the life-giving obedience of the Word, and a warning that she must 'keep and spend' the treasure entrusted to her on behalf of everybody. Her response is a highly inspired hymn of praise to the Holy Trinity and a warm prayer that she may be 'clothed in eternal Truth' and hasten onwards during her lifetime in the intoxicating light of most holy faith.

Catherine's contemporaries did not miss the importance of her 'book', and Latin translations were soon made in order to draw it to the attention of the learned despisers of the 'vulgar' language. Soon after the art of printing began to be practised in Italy, the first printed edition of the *Dialogue* was issued in the original language of Siena. Translations into the various languages then beginning to take shape in Europe soon ensued, together with new editions in Italian and in Latin, down to our time.[2]

THE LETTERS

Catherine's *Letters* amount at present to 381, but it is not impossible that more might be found in old convent libraries or elsewhere. In any case, the current collection is one of the most remarkable from the fourteenth century.

When did Catherine begin to send her messages? Probably about 1367 or not long after, when her activity in favour of the sick and the poor, and as peacemaker between rival families, attracted attention, and a group of followers began to gather round her.[3]

As to the last ones there is no doubt: Catherine dictated them until February 1380 or later, not long before her death. It is certainly very difficult to place the *Letters* in chronological order because very few are dated; some have references to well-known events, which enables us to give them an approximate date, but most bear no hint at all about time.

Catherine normally starts with a greeting and a wish:

In the name of Jesus Christ crucified and of sweet Mary. Dearest ... in Christ the sweet Jesus. I, Catherine, servant and slave of the servants of Jesus Christ, write to you in his precious blood, desiring. . . .

Catherine's wish for the person to whom she writes is the subject of the letter. She may want him or her to be constant in faith, warm in charity; to practise humility or temper justice with mercy; to be courageous in fighting abuse or patient in bearing offence. And we might be shocked or puzzled on reading that she wants her disciples to be 'nailed heart and soul to the cross'. Then Catherine will explain the motives for that wish: the advantages to be found in a particular behaviour and the disadvantages in its opposite. The close of the letter is normally a recall to its starting wish:

... and this is why I said that I wanted you to ...

and the concluding invocation:

Sweet Jesus, Jesus Love

brings back the reader to its heading.

The *Letters* provide us with a true understanding of Catherine's mind and character, and of the atmosphere, both natural and supernatural, in which she is immersed.

Concern for great problems such as the Hundred Years War or the Great Schism does not prevent her from being aware of everyday events, such as that of a monastery in grave need of help, or of the situation of a sick member of her spiritual family.

War weighing heavily on the people, the defenceless victims of the soldiers' greed and violence, and bad government leading to rebellion, are frankly denounced to those who are responsible for them. The headings of her letters are not just words without meaning; Catherine writes in the name of Christ, not in her own, and her 'I want you to' is not the expression of her own will, but of what in her intimacy with God she has come to know as his own will. This explains how deeply felt reverence for the Vicar of Christ can join with straight speaking. Her first letter to Pope Gregory, starting with a desire that he may be a fruitful tree, is a lecture about how important it is for him to acquire sound virtues in order to forward his mission for the welfare of Christianity. He should overcome love of self and, could he dispose of a hundred thousand lives, willingly give them all away and imitate the Good Shepherd. Only a few months later will she present to him a plan of action for peace in a troubled world; her first concern is about his being firmly founded on virtue. And later on, when on his way to Rome Gregory is still uncertain whether to go on or come back, she will remind him that courage is his duty:

Every reasonable creature who wants to serve God must have constancy, fortitude and patience . . . lacking them, no one could be a servant of Christ; he would become the slave of his own sensuality . . . O most holy father, my sweetest daddy, open your mind's eye and make your understanding see: if every man needs virtue for the salvation of his own soul, how much more, having to nourish and govern the mystical body of holy Church, your bride, are you in need of constancy, fortitude, patience. You know that when you were first planted in the garden of holy Church you had to dispose yourself to resist by your virtue our chief enemies, the devil, the flesh and the world. . . . Now you are Vicar of Christ, and have been labouring and fighting for the honour of God and the salvation of souls, and the reform of holy Church, which means for you additional labour and suffering . . . Your load being heavier, you are in need of a hardier manly heart, not one to be afraid whatever may happen. You are well aware, most holy father, that as you took holy Church as your bride, you undertook to work on her behalf, expecting the contrary winds of many sufferings and troubles to oppose your fight on her behalf. Face such dangerous winds in a manly way with fortitude, patience and long-lasting perseverance, never turning back for fear: persevere and rejoice in storms and battles. Let your heart rejoice, then, because in the many adversities that have happened and are still happening, God's work is being well done, nor was it ever done in any other way. And so we see that persecution of the Church, or the tribulations a virtuous soul has to endure, end in peace, attained through patience and long perseverance.

Gregory should fight, and win his battle, with the weapons of love, like a kind father longing for his prodigal son to come back to him:

Peace, peace, most holy father! May it please your holiness to receive your children who have offended you, father. May your benignity overcome their wickedness and pride. You will not have to be ashamed to stoop down and pacify your wayward child. . . . Alas, father, no more war, no matter what the cost!

And, after all, the situation is not so bad:

As far as I have come to know, people here want to meet you as a father. (L, 252)

9

While the troops of the antipope stayed in Castel Sant'Angelo, Urban VI had sought refuge in Santa Maria in Trastevere, not so near to the Castello as St Peter's. After their surrender he went back to the Vatican barefooted, in a procession of penance and thanksgiving; Catherine did not fail to praise him for that:

I rejoice, most holy father, with cordial joy, that my eyes have seen God's will fulfilled in you, in the humble action so long neglected, the holy procession. How pleasant to God and unpleasant to the devils was it! They tried, in fact, to raise inward and outside obstacles. But devilish fury was smoothed down by angels. (L, 351)

Catherine has a true understanding of the various needs of human souls and knows how and when to praise or to blame, to spur or to soothe. An example of her soothing way is a letter to Francesco Malavolti, a member of her spiritual family. The affection of the disciple for his 'mamma' is without question, but he simply could not help, now and then, doing something of which she did not approve.

Dearest and more than dearest child in Christ, the sweet Jesus. I, Catherine ... write to you in his precious blood wishing to have you back in the fold with your friends, and feel as if the devil had stolen you, and prevented your being yourself again. I, a miserable mother, am in search of you, and ask others to search for you, so that I might carry you on the shoulder of grief, and of the compassion I feel for your soul. Open, then, dearest child, open the eye of your mind, clear it of darkness, be aware of your fault, not in confusion of mind, but with knowledge of yourself and hope in God's kindness. (L, 45)

With Raymond of Capua, her 'father and son' on whose virtue she could rely, Catherine is quite stern. Raymond had disappointed her expectations by failing to fulfil the mission entrusted to him by Urban VI: to go to the king of France in order to call him back to obedience to him instead of following Clement, the antipope; a mission that Catherine, in her loyalty to Urban, must have warmly wished to reach its aim. But Raymond, having been warned about killers on his way, had come back. Catherine's reproach is anything but mild: he has proved to be like a child enjoying sweet milk and refusing to chew hard bread:

10

You were not worth keeping on the battlefield, but were sent back, as a child, and you were only too willing to fly away, and rejoiced as for a gift at what God granted to your weakness. You, my naughty father, how blessed your soul and mine could have been if by your blood you had added one stone to holy Church for the sake of [Christ's] blood! We have matter for weeping to see that our scant virtue has not earned such a gift. (L, 333)

In another letter she insists that if he had felt fully responsible, he would have tried any means rather than renouncing his duty:

If you had been faithful, you would not have vacillated . . . instead, like a faithful son readily obeying, you would have gone in whatever manner you could have managed. And, if you could not go upright, you might have gone on all fours; if not as a friar, as a pilgrim; and, if you had no money, as a beggar.

Then, as is customary with her, Catherine calls herself responsible for Raymond's fault:

Such faithful obedience would have worked better before God and men's hearts than all our human prudence; my sins have prevented my finding it in you. (L, 344)

One of the hardest, or probably *the* hardest, piece of reproach in Catherine's *Letters* is that to the three Italian cardinals who were giving allegiance to the antipope. Their pretence about the invalidity of Urban's election does not hold, and they are well aware of it. But they lie because they are unwilling to submit to his efforts to bring the clergy, cardinals included, to a way of living in tune with their ministry. Catherine does not hesitate to call them liars:

O misery upon misery! O blindness upon blindness, preventing you from seeing evil, and damage to soul and body! Had you seen it, you would not have so easily parted from truth with slavish fear, under the sway of your passions: pride and a habit of disposing at pleasure of human delights. You could not endure, I do not say actual correction, but even a harsh word of reproof made you raise your heads. And this is the motive for your change, which shows the truth. In fact, before Christ-on-earth began to bite you, you acknowledged and revered him as the Vicar of Christ that he is.

But soon, love for the souls of the rebels and desire to bring them to repentance makes her add:

> I will make it my duty to bring you before God by tears and incessant prayer and share your penance, provided you consent to go back to the father; he, as a true father, is waiting for you, the wings of his mercy wide open. (L, 310)

Like Italians in general and Tuscans in particular, Catherine did not lack a sense of humour and knew how to make use of it.

During her stay in Avignon, a letter was handed to Pope Gregory XI warning him about the danger from poisoning which might be awaiting him in Italy. Its author was said to be 'a servant of God', but in fact the letter had been written by people who were interested in keeping the papacy in France. For Catherine it is simply ridiculous; the person who wrote the letter had better attend school and learn, rather than prove so childish. He is contradicting himself because, after praising Gregory's intention of bringing the papal see back to Rome, he tries to prevent his leaving under the fanciful threat of poison. A true 'servant of God', she says, would never try to dissuade anyone from a good action just because it implied personal danger. And after all, slow or fast acting poison, lasting for one day or one month or one year, can be purchased in France as well as in Italy, provided one has money. But the venom that Gregory's failing to fulfil his promise would sow in the hearts of men and women is far more destructive.[4]

On hearing of William Flete's refusal to respond to Urban's summons to come to Rome just because he is afraid he may lose his 'spirit' once out of the hermitage at Lecceto, Catherine reacts by making fun of him and his fears:

> Too loosely is the spirit attached if it can be lost by change of place. This sounds as if God had a preference for woods, and could not be found elsewhere in times of need. (L, 328)

Catherine's awareness of having been entrusted with a particular mission and of her responsibility for its fulfilment is given strong evidence in letters from Rocca d'Orcia:

> Great shame to the citizens of Siena to believe or fancy that we are staying in the lands of the Salimbeni, or wherever in the world, to make treaties . . . all I want to do, or want those who are with me to do, is to deal with how to defeat the devil and free

sinners from his grasp by emptying their hearts of hatred and bringing them to make peace with Christ crucified and their neighbours. Such are the treaties that we are making, and that I require whoever may be with me to make.[5] (L, 122)

No doubt: she is the leader of the little group trying to restore peace and civilized behaviour in a land, the Val d'Orcia, badly upset by family rivalries, and it is up to her to decide what to do or not to do. As for her loyalty to her city, shame on the Sienese who might doubt it!

A letter to Raymond relating Catherine's assistance to a man sentenced to death is a remarkable witness to her power to communicate her own sentiments. A double thread is running all through the letter: the power of the blood of Christ to transform evil into good, and of his love to foster nuptial love.

The man was furious; he could not accept being deprived of life while still in his prime. Catherine visited him in prison, soothed him, led him to share her own view of death as the blessed moment when the soul is to join in the wedding banquet of union with God. She waited for him on the scaffold, in intense prayer, helped him to lay down his neck on the block:

Down, to the wedding feast, my sweet brother! Soon shall you be in everlasting life!

Then, his bleeding head in her hands, she says her imperious 'I will!' and is granted a vision of the man's soul entering the side of Christ, bathed in his own blood which has been given redeeming power by loving union with the blood of the Redeemer. The bridal motif has its final, most delicate touch, as the happy soul turns back to thank Catherine:

He made such a gesture as might draw a thousand hearts, but this is not surprising, since he was already savouring divine sweetness. He turned back like a bride coming to the door of her bridegroom's, who turns and bows her head to thank her escort. Once he had safely entered, my soul rested in peace and quiet.[6]

While Catherine was still in her teens, her mother had tried her best to dissuade her from practising hard penances which, she thought, would soon kill her. Catherine had normally defeated her, which did not prevent their being truly fond of each other, each in her own way, as Catherine aimed at spiritual progress, and Lapa at material welfare. Catherine's reproach to Benincasa, her brother, then in Florence, shows how she felt about Lapa:

> I have seen your ingratitude grow to the point that, let alone giving her support, which I know you could not do ... even of words you have been sparing. You have not considered her labour in giving you birth and the milk she gave you from her breast, and how she toiled in rearing you and the others. (L, 18)

Catherine, however, does not spare reproach when she feels that Lapa fails to understand that her daughter is coming and going not at her own pleasure, but in order to fulfil a precise duty. Thus, when her delayed return from Avignon causes unfriendly gossip which makes her mother a little too nervous, Catherine does not conceal her disappointment in finding that she is so far from sharing her mission and cannot accept its drawbacks, though she was not bothered when her sons left her just to earn money:

> You, as a kind and sweet mother, should be pleased, not displeased in bearing any kind of toil for the honour of God and for your salvation and mine ... I remember you could do so for the sake of temporal goods, when your children left you to get material wealth. . . . This means that you love better what I got from you, your flesh in which you clad me, than what God gave me.

Then she takes care to smooth down the reproach by a piece of good news:

> be comforted, now, for the sake of Christ crucified, ... Soon shall we be coming. . . . (L, 240)

The delay had been caused by the illness of a member of the company whom she certainly could not have left halfway, all alone, in Genoa. Catherine loved all her followers dearly and felt responsible for their welfare. To Bartolomeo Dominici who was having troubles from the evil spirit, she wrote:

> If the devil were to trouble your conscience, tell him to come and argue with me ... a mother has to answer for her children! (L, 204)

When she felt that her life was approaching its end she prayed to God:

> I recommend to you my most beloved children and beg you,

supreme eternal Father, should it please you to draw me from this vessel and never make me come back, do not leave them orphans, but visit them with your grace . . . I offer and recommend to you my most beloved children, because they are the soul of my own soul. (P, XXVI)

THE PRAYERS

The last quotation brings us to the comparatively small collection of Catherine's *Prayers*: no more than 26. The person who collected them took care to warn the reader that the ones included are only a few of the many which Catherine said in ecstasy, which anybody might have easily guessed. They afford a precious opening into her intimacy with the Godhead. Catherine did not dictate them, she simply used to pray aloud and at a certain moment her disciples realized that what she said was worth keeping and began to write down her words. According to the date recorded, this happy discovery was made in the summer of 1376, during Catherine's stay in Avignon. The last prayer is said to have been uttered at the end of January 1380, a few months before she died.

The beginning of the prayers is normally straightforward:

O all-powerful Father, eternal God . . .

High, eternal Trinity . . .

O Trinity eternal, you fire and abyss of charity . . .

soon giving way to a consideration of God's kindness to humankind: the creation of man after his own image, the redemption and, most amazing, God's unceasing loving care for his beloved creatures, no matter what their misbehaviour.

O God eternal, O God eternal, have pity on us! And should you say, high eternal Trinity, that pity breeding mercy belongs to you . . . I acknowledge it is so, since only out of pity did you offer the Word, your only-begotten Son, to death for our redemption. Such pity sprang from the fountain of your love which had moved you to create your creature. (P, VIII)

Whenever the mind is brought face to face with God's mystery it cannot but experience its own incapacity to penetrate its depths unless he gives it special enlightenment:

O God eternal, high and eternal magnitude! You are great but I am small, and therefore my lowliness cannot rise to your height, except as far as desire and intellect together with memory rise above the low level of my human condition and in the light you have given me from your light come to know you. (P, XII)

When praying Catherine is never alone before God: the interests of the whole world are always present to her:

How could I enjoy being saved if your people were to die, and I saw darkness rise in your Church, which is light itself? (D, XIII)

Her concern for the great human family suggests familiar words:

High eternal Trinity, inestimable love! If you call me daughter, I say to you high eternal Father! And, as you give yourself to me in the communion of the body and blood of your only-begotten Son . . . so, inestimable Love, I beg you to give me the communion of the mystical body of holy Church, and of the universal body of the Christian religion, since in the fire of your charity I have come to know that on this food you want my soul to delight. (P, IV)

On the feast of the Annunciation Catherine first praises Mary's unique privilege:

O Mary, Mary, you shrine of the Trinity!

then she speaks as if she were calling her aside to whisper in her ear:

Mary, were you troubled with fear by the words of the angel? It does not seem, on my considering it in true light, that fear did trouble you, even though you showed some wonder and trouble. Well, then, what causes you to wonder? God's great bounty, of which you were made aware, and as you looked at yourself and found how unworthy you were of such grace, you were amazed. . . . Thus in your prudent questioning you show your profound humility and, as has been said, you were not afraid; you just wondered at God's infinite bounty and charity in comparison to the lowliness and littleness of your virtue. (P, XI)

The *Prayers* are evidence of how soundly both Catherine's spirituality and her actions rely on the truths of Christian faith. In the supernatural world she can stay and move as easily as in her own natural home.

It was lucky for Catherine of Siena, and for us, that she should have proved so slow in learning how to read and write; had she learnt in the normal way, she might have been told how to do it properly and, in the effort to conform to current rules, she might have failed to forge her own personal style, thus depriving her language of its originality and beauty. But Catherine ignored rules, because she ignored writing. She spoke. She did not write her messages: she spoke with people who might be far away, but were present to her, and her scribes kindly wrote down her words so that they might reach him or her to whom they were said. She could even imagine their posing questions to which she would respond:

... and, were you to ask, ... I would say ...

Being free of conventional rules, her writings keep the natural spontaneity of the spoken language while her mind, unconscious of the slowing down of a pen, works at full speed.

SOURCES AND STYLE

As Raymond of Capua relates in his *Legenda*, Catherine once said to him that whatever she had come to know about the way to salvation she had not learnt from man or woman, but directly from the Lord Jesus Christ, either inwardly inspiring or visibly appearing and speaking to her as people normally speak to one another (*Life*, 84). No doubt she told the truth. But in reading her works we cannot help sensing the presence of various sources, such as Thomas Aquinas or Augustine and, most frequently, Holy Scripture. How can their presence be accounted for?

The liturgy and the sermons that Catherine heard at St Dominic's are no doubt chiefly responsible for her knowledge of texts which she certainly did not read. Conversation with her followers, which included distinguished lay members, Dominicans and other religious, must not be undervalued. At any rate, whatever entered Catherine's mind from outside merged with her own thoughts: a faculty of which she could, and did, freely dispose. Catherine does not bother about wording: she grasps the meaning and the idea springs up naturally, so naturally that every now and then one might not realize that she is quoting. But even when the quotation is intentional, it is not literal, which it could scarcely be, since it is given as presented by memory. Besides, Catherine has no problem about joining together different passages, as in the following:

> I must not turn back and abandon the ploughed ground as if we were ploughing at the request of this or that; then darnel would come and choke the wheat. (L, 250)

This fusion of three gospel passages is very effective. The warning 'once the hand is laid on the plough no one who looks back is fit for the kingdom of God' (Luke 9:62) is both a clear statement of Catherine's will to stay where she is and of the legitimacy of such will: she has not been working for material profits but for the kingdom of God and her work will be lost if she turns back before time. Why? Because darnel would come and spoil the crop. But this little seed, which in its own place (Matt 13:24–30, 36–43) was meant to imply that good and bad human beings will coexist on earth till the end of time, is even more evocative because it is also made a substitute for the choking thorns in the parable of the sower (Matt 13:22), and by the implication of the presence of its own evil sower who would not fail to come, if Catherine gave way, and spread discord by choking the good seed of peace she had been sowing.

The passage just quoted also affords an example of Catherine's way of condensing her messages in the fewest possible words. The speedy succession of thoughts as well as her natural bent for the essential prevent her indulging in particulars of little importance.

This is particularly to be noticed in her rich usage of imagery, which is never superfluous or ornamental; Catherine aims at the very core of the image she will use to express a reality of a different order; she catches what makes it what it is: its truth. Catherine's extremely concise style together with the depth of her thought can make it difficult to understand some of her passages in their full meaning; a hasty reading will be of little or no use with her: some passages have to be read over and over again, but the prize is worth the trouble.

THE TRANSMISSION OF CATHERINE'S WORKS

Catherine could not be unaware of the importance of her works. Her messages had been sent to all sorts of people in the name of Christ crucified and Mary, his dear Mother, and the *Dialogue* recorded the truth as revealed by the Godhead to her in the ecstasy of her soul, which truth she had been warned not to keep for herself, but to share with others. As regards the *Prayers*, we do not know whether she knew that her followers had been writing down words that she had not said to men or women.

In February 1380, about two months before she died, Catherine wrote to Raymond:

> I ask you for the book and any writings of mine you might find – you and Fra Bartolomeo, and Fra Tommaso and the Master – to take them in your hands and do with them whatever you may deem best for God's honour, together with Messer Tommaso; in them I used to find some comfort. (L, 273)

The five revisers found nothing to object to, and handwritten copies of Catherine's writings began to spread in Italy and all over Europe.

The *Dialogue* was soon translated into Latin to make it palatable to scholars who despised the newly-born 'vulgar' vernacular languages, and also to make it known beyond the Alps, Latin being still commonly used all over Europe. Only a few years after the art of printing had begun to flourish in Italy, while printers were busy chiefly with the Bible and the works of the great classics, Azzoguidi issued the first printed edition of the *Dialogue* (Bologna, 1472/75). The first edition of the Latin translation was made by Bernardino de Misintis (Brixiae, 1496). Translations into modern languages followed and continued to appear from the sixteenth century to our time. The *Dialogue* can be read today, as well as in Italian, in English, Flemish, French, German, Hungarian, Japanese, Polish, Portuguese and Spanish, and translations into other languages are being made.

A small collection of the *Letters* (31) was printed by Fontanesi (Bologna, 1492), and this was soon followed by a beautiful volume containing 353 letters, collected and printed by Aldo Manuzio (Venice, 1500). The Aldine edition provides two groups of the *Letters* according to their addressees: first come the letters sent to ecclesiastics, from Popes to simple religious, then those addressed to lay people, starting with kings and queens and descending to artisans or the members of Catherine's own family. The same order was given in the complete edition of Catherine's works edited by Girolamo Gigli in the first decades of the eighteenth century, his aim being to prove, through Catherine, that the language of Siena was as good as, or maybe better than, the more generally appreciated language of Florence. Nicolò Tommaseo made an effort, only partly successful, to present the *Letters* in chronological order (1860); his numbering is still generally used in Italian editions. E. Duprè-Theseider was better prepared for this hard task, but he could only publish the first volume of his critical edition (1940), which included 88 letters dictated from 1367/74 to the end of 1376. Complete translations of the 381 letters can be found in French, Hungarian and Spanish. The first volume of a translation into English that will include all the *Letters* was issued in 1988. A limited number of them can be read in English, German, Polish and Portuguese.

The *Prayers* were first printed by Aldo Manuzio together with the *Letters*, and reproduced in Gigli's edition of Catherine's works. Then they seem to have been ignored until 1919 when they were first issued as an independent volume, in a French translation, which attracted attention to the small but precious collection of Catherine's conversation with the Godhead. It was published in Italian with the addition of prayers excerpted from other writings of hers. A critical edition giving the Italian and Latin texts on facing pages was published in 1978 and afterwards translated into English, French, German, Polish and Spanish.

During the rather long period between Catherine's time and ours she has never been unpublished, as attested by the various editions of her works. A particular revival of interest both in them and in her activity can be observed in the last hundred years. It was partly fostered by the criticism of R. Fawtier, a French scholar who refused to admit Catherine's authorship of her writings, and doubted the objectivity of her early biographers. Since criticism encourages a response based on critical research, in 1936 Siena University founded a chair of Studi Cateriniani which produced critical editions of biographical sources. Its activity was unfortunately interrupted by the Second World War. Meanwhile a critical edition of the *Letters* was promoted by the Historical Institute in Rome; its first volume was issued in 1940. Later on critical editions of the *Dialogue* (1968, 1995) and of the *Prayers* (1978) were produced by the Centro Nazionale di Studi Cateriniani.

The results of such research have all been to Catherine's advantage, having led to an increased appreciation of the uncommonly high level of the thought and person of the uneducated young woman of Siena.

Notes

1. Until 1970 the Catholic Church numbered only 30 Doctors, all of whom had been members of the clergy. Then for the very first time in the history of Christianity, Pope Paul VI awarded this very distinguished title to two women: Teresa of Avila (29 September 1970) and Catherine of Siena (4 October 1970), who lived two hundred years before Teresa.
2. The very first translation of the *Dialogue* into a modern language is supposed to be that into Middle English made for the Bridgettine nuns at Syon Abbey and known as *The Orcherd of Syon* because of its singular division into seven parts, each consisting of five chapters, presented as 'alleys' for the sisters to walk in and enjoy the fruit of the trees. Wynkyn de Worde printed it in 1519. A critical edition was published for the Early English Text Society by Oxford University Press (1966).
3. Such is the opinion of E. Duprè-Theseider, who edited the first volume of a critical edition of the *Letters* in 1940, but was prevented from completing the edition because of his many commitments. Since his death (1976) the work for the critical edition has been resumed and is continuing, but it will still take time to be completed because of the number of letters and MSS.
4. Cf. L, 239.
5. The original presents a pun between *trattati* (treaties) and *trattare* (to deal, to speak of).
6. L, 273. This letter has been deemed sufficient in itself to qualify its author as a great writer; the human appeal of its dramatic character has made of it one of the most popular, and the mystery about the sentenced man has fostered research. Catherine, in fact, avoids writing his name, which she replaces by an anonymous 'the one you know of'. He certainly was not a common criminal and his guilt may have been involvement in some political plot. According to Caffarini, he was a citizen of Perugia, a city on no friendly terms with Siena at the time, and his name was Niccolò di Tuldo.

2

Catherine's search for truth

> God grant that I may always be
> a lover and a proclaimer of truth,
> and that for the sake of truth
> I may die. (L, 277)

At the beginning of the third part of his *Legenda Maior* Raymond of Capua states that, as Catherine was approaching the end of her life, her desire to be freed of her body and be given the gift to contemplate, unveiled, in her fatherland that supreme Truth which had been the object of her loving lifelong search was increasing day after day. He adds that, as if in answer to this desire, she was granted such a revelation about truth that she felt compelled to pass it on to others, so that she told her secretaries to be ready to write down whatever she might say. This is what they did, month after month, until Catherine's 'book' was completed.

The subject of the *Dialogue* is, then, truth; the truth that was shown to Catherine in that extraordinary enlightenment that she was granted 'about two years before her death'.[1] It is the same truth to which the Lord called her attention as she was just beginning to move in the ways of the spirit. In the first part of his *Legenda* Raymond relates how in the period between Catherine's admission to the Order of Penance of St Dominic and the Lord's call to her to go and share in the life of her family and of her city, on one of his frequent visits Jesus asked: 'Do you know who you are and who I am? If you know these two things you have beatitude in your grasp.' Then, without giving her time to think of a reasonable answer, he went on: 'You are the one who is not and I am He Who Am' (*Life*, 92).

Thus Catherine's innate desire for truth was granted the truest notion about Godhead in the name God himself had made known to Moses when sending him to rescue his people from slavery (Exod 3:14). But she may have been puzzled at being told that she 'was not'. She was certainly aware of being alive, hearing the sound of the Lord's words, seeing his lips move; aware of being free to stay or to go, to get up and walk out, or just remain seated where she was. Nevertheless she did not fail to grasp what the Lord was referring to, namely the nothingness of any being that cannot account for its own existence, having to seek for its principle outside itself; a void that is evidenced in the comparison with the plenitude of him who is Being itself and who causes whatever exists to exist. But the very consciousness of its own limits leads 'the creature which holds reason' to try and find out why it exists at all, and to begin to understand itself on becoming aware of the cause of its own existence.

Knowledge of truth is, then, the result of both knowledge of God and knowledge of self: the two are complementary and never to be separated, since knowledge of God alone, according to Catherine, might lead us to presumption, while knowledge of self without the assurance that our 'nothing' can rely on him 'who is' might prove a way to despair.

After imparting his instruction on the twofold knowledge, the Lord promised Catherine that, if she held to it, she would avoid all the snares of the enemy, and 'walk the royal road which leads to the fullness of grace and truth and light' (*Life*, 93).

Catherine did not hesitate to accept what the Lord kindly told her. She trusted him so well that his teaching about the importance of the twofold knowledge was to be the rock on which her doctrine would rest. But a problem immediately arose: why should 'He who is' care to call into existence beings of which he is absolutely in no need? There was only one answer to that question: nothing but love could cause him to do that. Thus the notion of creation as an act of love became the natural complement to the knowledge of God and of man, and gave it a constantly fresh appeal, a ceaseless cause of wonder. We can sense this persistent wonder in a prayer that Catherine spoke only a few weeks before she died:

Eternal Father, how did you create this creature of yours? I am indeed amazed at this, and truly see, after your showing me, that nothing caused you to do so except that in your light you saw yourself compelled by the fire of your charity to give us being. (P, IV)

Love as the cause of creation assumes a particular colouring when related to man, because God has made of him his own living portrait. In considering the creation as related in Genesis, Catherine remarks on the different value of God's life-giving words: the formula for creating sun, moon, stars, mountains and seas and all living beings is just 'Let there be . . . ' but when creating man he says: 'Let us make man in our own image, in the likeness of ourselves' (Gen 1:26). Catherine comments:

> This you did because you, eternal Trinity, wanted man fully to partake with you, high eternal Trinity. Therefore you gave him memory to keep the gifts of your bounty, thus sharing your power, eternal Father, and you gave him understanding that he might have a share in the wisdom of your only-begotten Son; and you gave him will that he might love what understanding saw and understood about your truth, thus partaking of the Holy Spirit's clemency. Who caused you to set man in such high dignity? Your inestimable love in looking at your creature within yourself which caused you to fall in love with it; and therefore you created it out of love so that it might savour your supreme eternal bounty. (D, XIII)

Before he can enjoy eternal bliss, man has to exert himself in his earthly life. The likeness of himself that the triune God has impressed on the human soul – one with three powers – is anything but static: the dynamism of memory, intellect and will mirrors the attributes of the three divine Persons, and God's love for his creatures must have its reflection in every man's love for his neighbour.

At the very beginning of mankind God said: 'It is not good that the man should be alone: I shall make him a helpmate' (Gen 2:18), and Adam was provided with company by having one of his ribs turned into a woman. Catherine seems to echo the Lord's disapproval of loneliness, but her idea of 'company' is quite different:

> You, high eternal Wisdom, have not set the soul all alone; you, on the contrary, have given it the company of the three powers, memory, understanding and will, and they are so closely united that whatever one wills the others comply with; so that, if memory applies itself to consider your gifts and unbounded goodness, intellect immediately wishes to understand them and will [wants] to move in its wake. Since you have not set it alone,

you do not want it to stay alone, without love of you and of neighbours. Then is it perfectly united, when it has such company: it is made one with you and one with neighbours by the union of love. (P, XXII)

Man is thus made to mirror the mystery of the triune God in the three powers of his one soul where memory portrays the Father in his power of holding in himself whatever exists; memory, likewise, has to keep what intellect has seen about Godhead, thus partaking in the wisdom of the Son; and will, after its model, sweet Holy Spirit, 'stretches out love's strong hand' to hold what understanding has come to know about God's bounty and fills memory with it.[2] Thus an insight into the mystery of man makes an opening to the bottomless mystery of the Holy Trinity, a mystery that is never absent from Catherine's mind. Its presence can be sensed in all her writings as the constant substratum of her thought; it bursts forth in the opening invocations of most *Prayers*:

O high, eternal Trinity . . .

I acknowledge, God eternal, high eternal Trinity . . .

O Trinity eternal, fire and depth of Charity . . .

In contemplating the mystery of the incarnation, Catherine invokes Mary as 'temple of the Trinity'. In another prayer she insists on the likeness of the triune God impressed in man:

O eternal Trinity, one God! You, Godhead, one in essence and three in persons, are a three-branched vine, if I may be permitted to make such comparison. You made man in your image and likeness so that by the three powers he has in one soul he might be similar to your trinity and unity. (P, XXIII)

The figure of the vine and its branches had been used by Christ himself to impress his disciples with the absolute necessity for them to be united to him, but Catherine seems to doubt whether it might be properly used when speaking of the Holy Trinity. However, images from the natural world fit her thought so well that she cannot avoid making use of them. Thus, when thinking of God the Father as enclosing within his mind all creatures, she sees him as a garden teeming with living power which blooms into flowers and bears fruit:

O eternal Trinity! In your light we come to know that you are that supreme eternal garden holding flowers and fruits within yourself, because you are the flower of glory, rendering glory to yourself.

Within the garden of your bosom, O eternal Father, was man enclosed. You drew him out of your holy mind like a flower distinguished by the three powers of his soul, and into each you have put the [living] plant, so that he may bear fruit in your garden and return to you with the fruit you gave him. (P, XIII)

Creation as an act of love implies providence. It is hardly possible to imagine that God might leave his beloved creatures to chance without keeping an eye on their welfare. Raymond of Capua states that Catherine's boundless confidence in divine Providence was one of the immediate results of her being taught the doctrine of the twofold knowledge. The Lord said to her: 'Think of me, child; if you do, I will not fail to think of you.' This meant, Raymond explains, that she should not worry about the welfare of either soul or body, because the Lord would care for both; he adds that the high regard she had for divine Providence caused her often to speak of it and to dedicate to this subject a large section of her 'book' (*Life*, 97–98).[3]

Here providence is first considered in a general way, as being aimed at the welfare of the whole of human society. It starts with man's being 'provided' with reason and free will, two precious qualities which he fails to appreciate. Then it is shown in God's promise of redemption, and in his keeping the flame of hope alive through the long sequence of men and events recorded in Old Testament. When time comes for the fulfilment of the promise, the good Physician's treatment of the sores in humankind punctually meets its needs:

Having lost the clothing of innocence and lacking shelter in virtues, man was starving and freezing to death ... But I, supreme Providence, provided for his needs. It was not any rightful deed or virtue of yours that compelled me: my own goodness did, and I gave you clothing through the sweet loving Word, my only-begotten Son. By stripping himself of life he clothed you with innocence and grace ... I also warmed him as my only-begotten Son – made known to you the fire of my charity through the opening in his chest ... My providence has given him food to comfort him while on his earthly pilgrimage

... and has made his enemies feeble so that nobody but himself can hurt him. And the road is made solid by the blood of my Truth so that he may reach his goal, my aim in creating him. And what food is this? ... It is the body and blood of Christ crucified, all God and all man ... You see, then, that my providence has provided comfort for him. (D, CXXXV)

However, God's loving care for his creatures is not satisfied with offering the means to salvation; he does not lose sight of any of them and provides help according to each one's needs. This particular Providence makes use of different ways according to the condition of every single soul. Sinners may be given remorse and disgust for their behaviour, or even be prevented from fulfilling their evil plans by physical hindrance, which will give them time to repent. God, in fact, 'can always pick a rose from our thorns' (D, CXLIII). The imperfect will be helped out of mediocrity by temptations laying siege to the citadel of their souls: a challenge to rouse their powers and fight. With the perfect the hand of providence is rather heavy: it prunes them by means of hardships, slander, rude mockery and reproaches, together with hunger and thirst, granted in proportion to each one's capacity to bear them. But to a soul who has come better to know and love God no pain smarts more than to see him offended.

I provide for them. How? By making myself known to them, making them see, in me, with great bitterness, the iniquity and misery of the world, and the damnation of souls ... so that they may be urged by the fire of desire to cry out to me with firm hope and the light of most holy faith, for help in such dire need. Thus by my divine providence I provide at the same time for the world by allowing the painful, sweet and anxious desires of my servants to compel me, and for them by nourishing them and making them grow, on this account, to more perfect union with me and greater knowledge. (D, CXLV)

So God allows himself to be solicited for the perfection of his creatures, a perfection that he himself has fostered. The idea that he should place so much weight on their entreaties is simply bewildering:

O eternal mercy, hiding the faults of your creatures! I do not wonder that you should say of those who get out from mortal sin and come back to you: 'I shall never remember that you ever offended me.' O ineffable mercy, I do not wonder that you should say so to those who free themselves from sin when about your persecutors you say: 'I want you to pray to me for them, that I may have mercy on them.' O mercy . . . ruling the whole world with your power! (D, XXX)

By the kind action of divine Providence helping him in his ascent, man is given a new nobility in addition to his having been created in God's image: he is now made one with Christ and is given a share in his mission:

These ones can indeed be said to be another Christ crucified, my only-begotten Son, because they have undertaken to perform his own task. He came as a peacemaker to put a stop to war, and reconcile man to me in peace through much suffering by the shameful death on the cross. They, likewise, go under the sign of the cross, by means of prayer and speech and a good and saintly life. (D, CXLVI)

Such people prove to be skilled fishermen by throwing their nets from starboard (John 21:6), the nets of boundless desire wanting to catch all the fish in the deep sea. They take such a large catch that they have to call for help in drawing the net to shore. And even if some fish may jump out of the net, they cannot leave their desire and prayers. The catch is, however, proportional to the perfection of the fisherman.

Perfection implies order in mind and body which, once achieved, makes the person like a well-tuned musical instrument producing sweet melodious sounds, so pleasant that people will be attracted and follow the player:

Be they willing or not, the wicked cannot help being attracted by so pleasant a sound, and many are so enticed by such a hook and instrument that they depart from death and come to life.

All saints have caught [souls] by means of this organ. The first to produce the life-giving sound was the sweet loving Word on assuming your humanity. And by humanity united to Godhead he made such a sweet sound on the wood of the cross, that he took hold of mankind, my child; he caught the devil by depriving him of the lordship he had had so long because of man's sin. All of you can learn how to play from this master. (D, CXLVII)

That creatures might be called to associate with God in his providential care of the world is more than anybody might expect. Such a call is a consequence of the divine image impressed in man and an addition to his natural dignity; it is, above all, the ideal opportunity for his need to love to be turned into action.

Apart from the honour that is given the perfect by their being used as good tools in God's hands for the fulfilment of his loving plan for man's salvation, they are also the object of his particular care, a care that is seen in those who renounce earthly possessions and put all their trust in God.

> Now I want to tell you just a little bit about my ways in assisting my servants, those who hope in me, in their bodily needs. . . . I never fail to help them, as long as they hope. I may well sometimes draw them to extreme limits, to make them better see and understand that I can and will help them, so that they may fall in love with my providence, and embrace true poverty as a bride. (D, CXLIX)

God is not short of ways. He may provide by inspiring a wealthy person to give alms to a very poor monastery; or by multiplying a few loaves of bread; or lending nourishing power to very poor food. He is particularly careful with regard to those who choose voluntary poverty, because they wage war on a greed for wealth, which is the chief cause of all the evil in the world, the worst enemy of God's providential plan. It breeds pride, avarice and robbery, hatred, violence; it turns the heart from the love and service of God to slavery of material things. The praise of poverty, which Christ practised all his life, forms the conclusion of the teaching about providence:

> This queen never has war in her kingdom; she has lasting peace and quiet. . . . The walls of her city are strong because they are not founded on earth or sand but on the living rock, Christ the sweet Jesus. . . . There is light, inside, and no darkness, because this queen's mother is the depth of divine charity . . . There is goodwill among all the citizens, love of neighbours; long-lasting perseverance and prudence . . . He who takes poverty, the sweet queen, for his bride, is given lordship of all such riches. (D, CLI)

In 1375 Catherine went to Pisa on a diplomatic mission. There she had her first sight of the sea as well as her first experience of sailing when she crossed to the island of Gorgona to visit a community of Carthusians. As the boat smoothly glided on the gentle support of the water – deep, bottomless waters teeming with life – and Catherine's eyes wandered farther and farther over the blue surface until it merged at the horizon with the azure of the sky, the idea of God's immensity and that of the loving presence of his Providence in the created world became one. God was the 'peaceful sea' providing shelter and food for numberless living beings. A letter she sent at the time to Fr Bartolomeo Dominici, then in Florence, is a good insight into her feelings:

> To you, most beloved and dearest father in reverence of the sweetest sacrament, and son in Christ Jesus, I, Catherine, servant and slave of the servants of Jesus Christ, write to comfort you in his precious blood, desiring to see you burnt and consumed in the fire of his most ardent charity, for I know that he who is burnt and consumed by such fire has no self-concern. And this is what I want you to do. I ask you to enter a peaceful sea, by that burning charity, a deep sea. This have I just found out – not that the sea is new, but it is new to me, in my soul's sensing it – in the words 'God is love'. And, as a mirror reflects a man's face, or the sun lights up the world, so these words present to my soul that everything is love, because all are made of nothing but love. This is why he says: 'I am God, love.' (L, 146)

Thus the 'novelty' of the sea opened Catherine's mind to a deeper understanding of the words 'God is love' (1 John 4:16) which were certainly not new to her. Likewise, the notion that the beauty of nature has God's love at its source should help us to understand that his whole behaviour towards us is ever prompted by love. We should behave – Catherine says – like one receiving a present from a friend: if friendship is genuine, he will not put so much store on the value of the gift as on the affection that causes his friend to give him a present at all. Such belief will spare us trouble when everyday events are not exactly what we should like them to be:

> Godhead, Godhead, eternal Godhead! . . . you are a peaceful sea where the soul that rests on you is fed and nourished through love's affection and union, by conforming its will to your high eternal will which only requires our sanctification. . . . O sweetest love! This appears to me as a genuine sign of their staying in you: their conforming to your will in your way, not their own. This is the best sign of their being clad in your will: that they should not consider events as being caused by the will of creatures but by your own will, and rejoice, not in prosperity, but rather in adversity, which they understand to be given by you out of sheer love. This is why they love it as well as they love your

creatures, all of which are good and therefore worth loving. (P, II)

The 'peaceful sea' as an image of God's boundless provident presence was to remain a favourite with Catherine. It runs through the hymn of praise concluding the *Dialogue* in which Catherine gives vent to her gratitude for the insight into the mystery of eternal Truth she has been granted:

> O Trinity eternal, O Godhead! . . . You, eternal Trinity, are a profound sea, so that the more I enter it the more I find, and the more I find the more I seek for you. You do not satiate, because the soul that feeds at its pleasure in your depth does not feel satiated: it always remains hungry for you, thirsty for you . . .
> O depth, O eternal Godhead, O sea profound. (D, CLXVII)

It is the natural tendency of Catherine's mind, whenever she thinks of one reality, to give it more emphasis by considering an opposed one. No wonder, then, she images the same reality in different or even contradictory ways. It is possible to read:

> God's Son . . . is the peaceful sea providing drink to all who have been at war and want to be reconciled with him. This sea pours out a fire that can warm any cold heart; it warms so well that all base fear is lost, and only perfect charity remains. (L, 144)

The soul could not be kindled by the fire of love if it had not been first given light to know what to love: God's fire sheds both light and warmth:

> O depth, O eternal Godhead, O sea profound! How could you have given me more than to give me yourself? You are a fire ever burning without consuming; you are a fire whose warmth burns away from the soul all selfishness; you are a fire removing cold; you shed light . . . Truly, this light is a sea; because it feeds the soul with you, the peaceful sea. In your light you have made me know your truth: you are that supreme light lending supernatural light to the mind's eye, so abundantly and perfectly that you make the light of faith brighter. In that faith I see that my soul is alive, and in this light it receives you, light . . .
> Truly is this light a sea, because it nourishes the soul in you, the peaceful sea . . . Its water is not troubled and therefore the soul has no fear because it knows the truth; it is so clear that it lets hidden realities be seen. It is a mirror, reflecting what you, eternal Trinity, let me know because, as I look into this mirror,

holding it with the hand of love, it makes me see me, your creature, in you, and you in me by the union that you made of your divinity with our humanity. (D, CLXVII)

The image of fire permeates one of Catherine's most beautiful and profound prayers, affording a good example of the constant presence in her mind of the basic twofold truth together with its consequence: love having to be offered to God by means of our neighbours. The first move is her usual bold spring upwards to the object of her desire:

Eternal Godhead, high eternal Godhead! O ever-blazing fire! You, eternal Father, high eternal Trinity, are the inestimable fire of charity. O Godhead, Godhead, who can show your bounty and magnitude? Your gift to man. And what is your gift to him? You, yourself, eternal Trinity.

Then she folds back as if in search of more power for her flight:

O God eternal, God eternal! You tell me to gaze at you, high eternal Godhead, so that by looking at you I may come to know myself, and have a better understanding of my lowliness as compared to your height and of your loftiness in comparison with my littleness. . . . O ever-burning fire, the soul that comes to know itself in you, wherever it may turn, finds your greatness even in the most trifling things, in all created beings, because in all of them it sees your might, your wisdom, your clemency . . .

And how do you want me, sweetest love, to look at me in you? You want me to consider your creating me after your image . . . You want, eternal Goodness, that I look at you and see that you love me and love me graciously so that I may likewise love all rational creatures, and that you want me to love and help my neighbours in their spiritual and bodily needs, as well as I can . . .

In your nature, eternal Godhead, I shall come to know my own nature. And what is my nature, inestimable love? It is fire, because you are nothing but fire of love and of such nature you have gifted man because in love's fire you have created him. (P, XXII)

The humbling contrast between God's infinite greatness and the limits of human nature gives way to the thought of the communion between Creator and creature: God is love, and the creature of his love is, also, love.

This is the truth Catherine was told by 'first sweet Truth', the unshaken basis of her doctrine, the lifelong object of her love.[4]

Notes

1. Cf. *Life*, 349.
2. Cf. P, I.
3. The 'Doctrine on Providence' is in fact so important that the *Dialogue* has sometimes been published under the title of *Book on Divine Providence*.
4. In *Summa Theologiae*, I, q. 16, a. 5, in answer to the question 'whether God is truth', Thomas Aquinas states that 'not only is truth in him, but he is truth itself, supreme first truth'. Catherine, the lover of truth, echoes his words in her favourite paraphrase for the name of God, 'gentle first Truth'.

3

Catherine and human nature

> I want you always to rest
> between day and night,
> by coming to know
> yourself in God and God in you. (L, 365)

In his speech at the closing session of Vatican II, Pope Paul VI (1963–78) stated that, while man is a mystery to himself, faith opens the way to a right understanding of human nature through knowledge of God. In fact, 'to know man, the real man, the whole man, one must know God', and he added: 'let us find a proof to this statement in the burning words of St Catherine of Siena: "In your nature, eternal Godhead, I shall come to know my own nature"'.[1] And his successor, John Paul II, refers to the same passage in his encyclical *Centesimus Annus*, where Catherine's words are the only quotation from a saint and a mystic.

Because of the antithetical teaching imparted to her about divine nature and humanity, Catherine's notion of man stands between the two extremes of nullity and excellence, because the same voice which had told her 'you are the one who is not' would ask her to admire the nobility and beauty of that same creature:

> Open your mind's eye and gaze unto me, and you shall see the beauty and nobility of the creature which holds reason in itself . . .

Besides, in addition to its native qualities, the same creature has been given the possibility of uniting with its Creator by the power of love:

and within the beauty I have given the human being by creating it after my own image and likeness, look at those who are clad in the nuptial robe of charity: they are united to me by love. I therefore tell you that, should you ask me who they are, I would answer . . . they are another myself, because they have lost and refused their own will, and have put on my own, uniting and conforming themselves to it. (D, I)

Does this imply that a little created being can rise to the height of Godhead? It can, in some way, since God first stooped down to his creature and gifted it with being in his own image and likeness, then united human nature to his own Godhead.

The divine likeness of the triune God impressed in man is seen by Catherine in the one human soul and its three powers: memory, understanding and will. The description of the creation of man (Gen 1:26) is the primary source for her understanding of such reality and for her way of expressing it:

O supreme Goodness, who made us after your own image and likeness out of sheer love, not saying 'Let there be' when you created man as when you made all other creatures, but you said: 'Let us make man in our own image, in the likeness of ourselves', O ineffable Love, so that the whole Trinity should consent, and you conformed him to the Trinity, eternal Godhead, in the powers of his soul.

The image of the living God impressed on that living being is not just a portrait: it implies similarity in life. This is how Catherine sees the reflection of the life of the divine Persons in the interaction of the three powers:

You gave him memory in conformity to you, eternal Father, who hold and keep whatever exists within your fatherhood: likewise did you give him memory so that he may hold and keep what the mind sees and understands about you, infinite Goodness, thus partaking of Wisdom, your only-begotten Son. You gave him will, Holy Spirit's sweet gentleness, which, when filled with your love, rises to grasp what intellect has come to know of your ineffable goodness. Thus, by will and love's strong hand are memory and affection filled with you. (P, I)[2]

The interaction of the three powers is given a full description in the *Dialogue*. Having been created by eternal Love, the soul has an innate tendency to love. Catherine calls it *affetto*, which

35

can be approximately translated as 'affection'. It is compared by Catherine to feet carrying the body; in the same way, affection moves the soul. It acts as a propeller and moves the powers to love, thus satisfying the basic need of the soul by giving it the food it feeds on. This is how the kind Lord explains to Catherine the workings of the soul's powers:

> The soul cannot live without love, it must always love something because it is made of love, having been created by me out of sheer love. This is why I told you about the affection's waking up the intellect as if saying: 'I have to love, because the food I feed on is love.' Then the intellect, sensing that it is being woken up by affection, rises as if saying: 'Since you are in need of loving, I will not fail to give you something to love.' And without delay it gets up and considers the beauty of the soul and the indignity following upon sin. (D, LI)

The awareness of the precious qualities it has been endowed with, and of its own ingratitude in spoiling them, leads the soul to consider God's great patience in waiting for it to come back to him. The remembrance of God's kind forbearance is the food offered to the intellect in its search for what to love; in savouring it the soul conceives displeasure for its own faults and desire of genuine virtues. By contrast, if sensuality were to entice one to love objects unworthy of loving, the eye of the intellect would turn in search of nothing but transitory realities, self-love, dislike of virtues and attachment to vice, with pride and impatience. Memory is in fact filled by what affection offers. Such love has a dazzling effect on the mind's eye which is prevented from perceiving anything but glimmers of light: the faint glimmers of pleasure coating vice and making it desirable. Such deceptive glimmers are in fact what leads man to do evil, his natural bent being towards good.

> Without such a glimmer man would never sin because, according to his nature, man cannot wish except what is good. But vice painted in the colour of self-interest can harm the soul. A blinded eye does not know the truth, and in its search for comfort and pleasure it wanders where they are not to be found.
> I have already told you that all worldly pleasures are poisonous thorns. So intellect is cheated in its sight, and will in loving what it should not, and memory in keeping it.

Is it possible to resist the enticement of evil so disguised? Yes it is, because man is free in his choice:

Free will is bound to affection, and can move it at its own pleasure, either in the light of reason, or without reason. Your reason is bound to me, provided free choice does not cut you off by unruly love.

We have to deal with two opposite tendencies, sensuality and reason: both may turn to our advantage if used in the right way:

Sensuality is a servant: it has been given to the soul to be at her service so that by means of your body you may practise virtues. The soul is free, having been freed from sin by the blood of my Son, and cannot be mastered unless it consents . . . Free choice is bound midway between sensuality and reason: it can turn to either as it chooses. (D, LI)

Of all the qualities God has given to his beloved creature, free choice is the most remarkable. It is a 'dowry', something not to be given away, but to be kept and made use of at any time. In presenting to one of her disciples the episode of the Canaanite woman asking the Lord to deliver her daughter from demonic possession, Catherine stresses the fact that he entrusted the recovery of the girl to the woman's choice:

In fact, wanting to show how much her faith pleased him, God entrusted the victory to her by saying: 'Be it done as you will' (Matt 15:28).

Upon this statement the praise of faith, and of her companions hope and charity – the three pillars on which the stronghold, the human soul, rests – follows quite naturally. But Catherine finds in the episode a good opportunity to insist on free choice, one of her favourite topics:

Here God's unbounded goodness makes us know the treasure he has given the soul: its own free choice, since neither devil nor any creature can compel one to commit a single mortal sin, unless one consents to it. O dearest child in Christ Jesus, consider with faith and true perseverance, that until death such words are being said to us. Know that as soon as a human being is created, God says: 'Be it as you will', which means: 'I make you free, that you may not be subject to anything, except myself.'[3]

Such thoughts draw from Catherine a warm praise of God's special kindness to man and a complaint for man's poor response:

O inestimable and sweetest fire of love, you show and make known the excellence of this creature, since all things you created for the service of your reasonable creature, and that creature you made that it should serve you. . . .

But we, miserable wretches, turn to loving the world with its pomps and pleasures, and because of such love the soul loses her lordship and becomes the slavish servant of sin. She has made the devil her lord. . . . But I want us to be in love with God, never forgetting that we were redeemed by the blood of the Lamb: a slave cannot sell himself or serve another master. We were not redeemed by gold or by the mildness of love, but by blood. (L, 69)[4]

Catherine could well speak of the power of will as she had experienced it personally. She was still in her teens when she summoned her large family, who wanted her to be married, and declared that she meant to keep her vow of virginity: they would sooner melt a stone than change her mind. And the family had to bend to her will (*Life*, 54).

The human soul, says Catherine, is like a stronghold with three doors – its powers – and some wicket-gates – bodily senses – through which enemies try to get in and possess that 'noble city'. Memory and understanding might be skilfully enticed and open their doors; will would not because free choice keeps the key of that door and is strong enough not to yield to alluring promises, provided it stays within the light of reason. Should it refuse this light, then love of pleasure and of self, pride, hatred and all their companions would flood in. Then understanding would be obscured and memory would cherish the remembrance of unlawful pleasures or of offences calling for vengeance (D, CXLIV). Still, free choice would have the power of getting the soul rid of its enemies. It would behave like a hand, first hurting, then healing the wound: the damage of its having yielded to alluring glitters can be cured by turning the mind's eye to pure light and the will to the warmth of authentic love:

Christ crucified, keeping the great warmth in the basin of our humanity, opens to us the profound fire of God's inestimable charity in the glory of divine nature united with human nature. This Word, Christ crucified, when looked at, throws such warmth and light, as to dissolve darkness and dry up the humidity of self-love; his light dissolves darkness and supernatural light is infused in the intellect. (L, 343)

God has made man free, and powerful over himself. (L, 177)

This does not mean that he may squander this treasure: the power he has been given is that of being his own judge by 'rising above himself' to the level of objective justice there to sit on the chair, his own conscience, and behave as a judge at trial, with clear discernment about what is right and what is wrong: he has to be, at the same time, both the person on trial and the impartial judge. For the power he has been given he is responsible to the Giver, to himself and to the universe which is seen as centred on him:

> In my wisdom I ordered and rule the world in such a way that nothing is missing, and nobody could add to it. I perfectly provided for soul and body, being compelled not by you, since you did not exist, but by my own kindness. By myself was I compelled to make heaven and earth, sea, and fire and water to temper contraries with each other, and the sun to prevent your staying in darkness: everything was made and disposed so as to provide for man's needs. The sky adorned with birds, the earth yielding fruit, the sea adorned with fish: everything did I make with great order and providence.[5]

The universe is, then, seen as the place expressly planned for man to live in and grow to perfection:

> After creating every good and perfect thing, I created the rational creature in my image and likeness, and put it in this garden. But the garden, because of Adam's sin, sprouted thorns where there had been fragrant flowers, the sweet purity of innocence. Everything was obedient to man but, because of his sinful disobedience, he found rebellion in himself and from all creatures. The world grew wild, and so did man, this other world. (D, CXL)

God is too fond of his creatures to allow them to be ruined, and provided the means to restore the beautiful garden he had expressly made for man by sending his own Truth. The Word incarnate watered the soil with his blood, uprooted the poisonous plants of self-love and set in their stead the gifts of the Holy Spirit. But, still, man will not behave as the wise gardener he should be. Hence God's complaint to Catherine:

> You could never tell how great is man's ignorance: he has no wisdom, no knowledge; he has deprived himself of it by hoping in himself and relying on his own knowledge. You silly man, don't

you see that you have not acquired it by yourself? My bounty gave it to you, providing for your need. (D, CXL)

Ignorance is too sad a fault in the creature which has reason as its hall-mark: to refuse evidence and fail to acknowledge one's limits is just foolish.

Love of self is the venom which has poisoned the whole world because it is opposed to the essential precept of charity. To refuse true love is to make oneself nothing. Christ said: 'When two or three are gathered in my name, there am I in the midst of them' (Matt 18:20). These words are commented on thus in the *Dialogue*:

> The man who is alone is afraid, but if he had a companion he would not fear . . . If one has no companion I cannot stay in the midst; such a man is nothing, because he who abides in self-love is alone; being cut off from my grace and from love of neighbours he has deprived himself of me by his own fault and turns to nothingness because I, and no other, am He who am. Therefore the man who stays alone, bound in his self-love, is held of no account by my Truth and unacceptable to me. (D, LIV)[6]

When love is lacking there is no gathering of human beings and no 'midst' for the Lord to stay in, but he provides the means to enforce the observance of the law of love by making exchanges of help necessary for human life:

> Easily could I have endowed men with what they needed, both for their souls and bodies; but I wanted them to be in need of one another, so that they should be my ministers and administer the graces and gifts they have received from me. In fact, be they willing or unwilling, they cannot avoid practising the acts, at least, of charity. (D, VII)

Since the universe is planned for the welfare of man it is not surprising that nature should contribute to his growth in the practice of love by its own variety, alternating fertile and barren land, abundance and scarcity of raw materials. Thus the unequal distribution of natural resources, the cause all along in the history of mankind of harsh rivalries and strife, is to be seen, within God's plan, as a clever contrivance to make man obey the law of love:

> You see, then, that to make them practise the virtue of charity I made them my ministers and placed them in different situations and at various levels. This is to show you that in my home there are many mansions and that all I require is love. (D, VII)

Unequal distribution of talents at a personal level is aimed at the same end:

> Open your heart wide, and open your mind's eye in the light of faith, to see how lovingly and providentially I created man and set him in place so that he may come to enjoy my supreme eternal bliss. . . . In this mortal life, while you are on your pilgrimage, I have bound you in the bonds of charity: be he willing or not, man is bound by it. Should he try to untie his affection by refusing to love his neighbours, necessity would still bind him. Therefore, to compel you to practise charity in deeds and affection, should you because of your sins fail to consent by your affection, you are compelled in any case to act in its way – I provided the means by not giving each single person the abilities to supply all the needs of human life, but this person has one and that another, so that all should be impelled to have recourse to others in their needs. You can see, in fact, how a craftsman resorts to a workman, and a workman resorts to a craftsman: the one is in need of the other because he cannot do what the other can. Likewise the clergyman and the monk are in need of the layman, and the layman of the monk: they cannot do without one another. And so it is for every other thing.
>
> Could I not give everything to everyone? Why, yes! But in my providence I wanted to ensure that they should humbly ask for one another's help and be compelled to practise charity in deeds and in good will. (D, CXLVIII)

> Once you have come to know my goodness, you come to love it . . . not for self-advantage, but by means of virtue which is conceived for my own sake . . . and given birth in your neighbours . . . Whoever loves me in truth, tries to help his neighbours and it could not be otherwise, since love of me and love of neighbour are one thing, and as much as the soul loves me, it loves him, because love of him comes from love of me. This is the means I offer you to practise and test your virtue . . . The soul in love with my Truth never stops helping the whole world, in general or in particular, little or great, according to the disposition of those who receive and the ardent desire of the giver.

Though our desire to help should extend to the whole world since desire is boundless, almost infinite, our good will should aim practically at objects within our reach:

Teaching or advising loyally, without reference to one's own interests, giving the edifying example of a good, saintly and honest life. (D, VII)

Returning God's love is all that we are required to do, and it is not a heavy task, since to love is innate to man. But having to return it through our fellow beings may cause some difficulties: our good will to help may meet with indifference, ingratitude, misunderstanding. Love's two-edged sword may find itself turned on the wrong side, the side of hatred. Besides, the very beauty of the universe where we were placed by the Creator's kindness might afford such pleasure as to make us forget who provided for it. And laziness or sensuality might induce us to centre love on self.

This is why man has to stay in the beautiful garden as on a battlefield where he must fight bravely. To do so he has to know what to fight for; he has to understand his own truth, and why and how that truth is worth fighting for. If he lends an ear to the inmost desires of his soul he will repeat, with Catherine, Augustine's words: 'You made us for yourself, God, and our heart is restless until it can rest in you.'

To be made aware of this desire is to learn how innate our need for faith is. Catherine compares our natural disposition to love to the wax of a candle: once the candle is lighted, the wax will feed the flame, but unless it has a wick inside, the candle will not burn at all.

This is how Catherine is made to understand this truth:

The material you are made of is love, because I created you out of love, and therefore you cannot live without love.

Such being, given you out of love, has been disposed [to love] in holy baptism, which you receive by virtue of the blood of the Word. Without that you could not partake of this light, and would be like a candle with no wick inside: it could not burn and be lit. Likewise, unless you had received in your soul most holy faith, the wick that can share the flame, thus uniting the grace you receive in baptism with the natural bent of your soul which I created to be disposed to love: as I told you, it has such a bent towards loving that it cannot live without it: its food is love. (D, CX)

To satisfy the soul's hunger, love cannot restrict itself to material objects, however good. The soul is hungry for the infinite. Our very reason, while throwing light on objects within its range, points to what is beyond that. This is where faith must come and help by lending its 'wick' to the flame to burn bright. Without the light of reason we could not love at all; without the light of faith love would not reach perfection. This is why Catherine prays:

> Love, sweet love! Open our memory, that we may take into ourselves God's great goodness, and cling to it and understand it, because through understanding we come to love, and by loving we are united and transformed into charity, the loving mother. (L, 41)

Because of the interaction of intellect and will, better knowledge of the object to be loved leads to increased desire for it, and desire thus increased will beg of understanding clearer knowledge of its object. This is why in the unitive stage of love, where it reaches its perfection,

> then the eye of the mind is rapt in the fire of my charity – says the Lord – and in that charity they receive supernatural enlightenment, and in this light they love me, because love follows upon understanding, so that the more one knows the more he loves, and the more he loves, the more he comes to know. This is how they feed each other. (D, LXXXV)

Faith is not a surplus; it is the response to the request of the human soul for a worthy object to satisfy its own need to love, and satisfy at the same time its desire for truth. Full appeasement can only be found in God, 'sweet first Truth', and in his loving plan for man whom he created to make him share his own eternal bliss. This plan he is so fond of as to want it to be fulfilled at any cost, even if he, himself, should have to pay for man's misdoings. The ideal image of this creature, as conceived in the divine mind, is so beautiful that he is 'foolishly' in love with it.

> O eternal Father, uncreated charity! I am full of wonder, having come to know, in your light, that you saw and knew me and all rational creatures before you gave us being ... and that you knew that sin was to hinder your truth by preventing your creature from attaining the purpose of its creation. You also saw, eternal Father, the sufferings that would ensue for your Son to restore mankind to grace and achieve your truth in us ...
>
> Well, eternal Father, how did you come to create this creature of yours? I am quite amazed since I clearly see, on your showing me, that for no other motive did you do this, except that in your light you saw the fire of your charity compelling you to give us

being, in spite of the iniquities that we were to commit against you, eternal Father. [Your own] fire, then, compelled you. O ineffable love, though in your light you saw all the iniquities your creature was to commit against your infinite goodness, you pretended not to see, and set your eyes on the beauty of your creature with whom you fell in love like a fool or one drunk with love, and in love you gave it being in your image and likeness. (P, IV)

It can be hard, sometimes, to be aware of that beauty in our daily intercourse with people, unless we look at them in the perspective of God's creative love. It is, says Catherine, as if one saw his own image reflected on the surface of a fountain: he should love the fountain revealing his own image, rather than the image. As we look for our own identity in the boundless sea of divine essence, we find our true image in him, and in ourselves, God's image, we find him.

Think, my dearest children, that in no other way could we see our dignity, nor the flaws which lessen the beauty of our souls, unless we go and see ourselves reflected in the peaceful sea of divine essence.

The soul that sees itself reflected in it comes to understand itself as the fruit of his burning love, and similarly all human beings.

Then he turns his desire to love himself in God, and God in himself, like a man looking at himself in the fountain and seeing his own image in it, and on seeing it he is pleased and rejoices. If he is wise he will first be prompted to love the fountain, then himself because, had he not seen himself, he could not have loved, and been pleased, nor could he have removed from his face the smudge he had seen in the fountain. (L, 226)

To remove the smudge and restore beauty in the soul is not an easy task; it is the hardest part of the struggle to be fought for perfection, since it does not have to deal with outside adversaries who may come and go, but with ourselves. But there is no way we can avoid it. We must feel responsible to God for his gifts: 'being and whatever rests upon being', as Catherine says; to ourselves to whom such talents were entrusted in order that we should make the most of them, and not hide them in the soil; to human society to whose welfare each one has to contribute. But no one can give real help to his neighbours by teaching, example and prayer, unless he has first helped himself by acquiring virtue. (D, I)

How are virtues to be acquired?

Know, dearest daughter, that by persevering in humble, continuous, faithful prayer, a human soul acquires, with true perseverance, every virtue. This is why one must persist and never leave off praying . . . (D, LXVI)

If this is the way to acquire virtue, one might say that it is an impossible way to follow: not even a monk can pray without interruption, let alone lay people.

The key to the solution of this difficulty is offered by the distinction between three kinds of prayer: vocal, mental and continuous. Vocal prayer, by means of psalms or particular formulas, makes the first step. Catherine reacts against the popular custom of repeating such formulas as 'Hail Mary' or 'Our Father' quite a number of times – hundreds, thousands – with no other concern than to reach the self-proposed number: mechanical repetition of words is void of spiritual profit. But, if the mind rests on the meaning of the words, and savours them, the soul can rise to the second level, that of mental prayer. Here one must be careful not to bother about the words, and open oneself to the inspiring visit of divine grace. Then the Holy Spirit will throw flashes of light on the mystery of God and of man, opening to the mind's eye the meaning of the incarnation and passion of the Word of God as a challenge to love, in return for his love for mankind.

At this point the soul reaches the third level of prayer, that of good will and constant desire which, Catherine says, is continuous prayer:

Everybody, in a way suited to his personal situation, is bound to exert himself towards the welfare of human souls, according to [God's] holy will. Whatever one does, by words or deeds, on behalf of his neighbours, is actual prayer even though one should reserve some time and place just for prayer. Apart from the prayer which he is bound to make, whatever he does, either for the love of neighbours or on his own behalf, is prayer. As Paul, my glorious herald, said: 'He who does not stop doing good deeds, does not stop praying.' This is why I told you that actual prayer could be performed in many different ways together with mental prayer, because actual prayer, when performed as has been said, is prompted by charity, which is continuous prayer.[7]

O, how sweet to the soul and pleasant to me – says the Lord – is holy prayer made in the house of knowledge of self and knowledge of me, lovingly opening the eye of the mind in the light of faith to my overflowing charity, made visible by my visible only-begotten Son, who showed it to you in his blood. (D, LXVI)

Our stay in this house where light is thrown on our knowledge of God and of self finds expression in the image of fire and sparks:

O most ardent, ever-burning fire, you are fire indeed! . . . and, as a spark is bred by fire, likewise do we receive life from our first principle. And this is why he said: 'I am fire, and you just a spark.' Then, do not allow your soul to rise in pride. Act like a spark, first rising, then coming down. This means that the first movement of our holy desire should tend towards knowledge of God and desire of giving him honour; then, once we have risen, let us come down to know our misery and negligence. O, you who are asleep, wake up! And we shall be humbled by finding ourselves in the depths of his charity. (L, 70)

Sparks, being extinguished almost as soon as they are lit, are good reminders of the brevity of human life, but their going upwards and downwards can also depict our soul rising to the contemplation of Godhead then coming down to the consciousness of our own limits. This is what Catherine calls 'the office of the servant' who brings messages to his master and comes back with his answers; it can be done on our own behalf and on behalf of others:

I, Catherine, . . . want to do for you the office of a servant for his master: he is always taking and bringing back. Likewise do I want always to take you to the presence of our sweetest Saviour and, in thus doing, be granted by his ineffable love the grace to comply with the other task of the servant which is to bring back; that is to say, to come down, and attain to the grace of knowing ourselves and God. (L, 30)

To do this service we shall be particularly urged by our staying in the deep warmth of charity from which we, the minute sparks, take our heat and light:

Open, open your hearts wide to receive neighbours in love and desire ... O dearest and sweetest brothers, let us get up from sloth, and hasten to run along the way of truth, but let us hasten to run as dead ones, without allowing the ingratitude of creatures to keep us back. Sow, sow the word of God, return the talents that were entrusted to you. (L, 70)

To stay in the warmth of charity is to persist in prayer:

Then, in a manly way shall the soul spur itself with prayer, this mother. (D, LXVII)

Prayer breeds charity, and charity is the mother of all virtues. The task of this mother in rearing her children is anything but easy: virtues are to be acquired through their opposites; they are conceived in prayer but cannot be said to be born and alive until they have come to confront their opposites:

All virtues are tested and given birth in neighbours; likewise the wicked give birth to all vices in their neighbours. You can see that humility is tested [in the confrontation] with pride, which means that a humble person puts off pride, since the proud cannot harm the humble, nor can the infidelity of the wicked who do not love me or hope in me, hurt those who are loyal to me, or lessen faith and hope in those who have conceived them for my sake; on the contrary, these virtues are strengthened and tested in the love of neighbour ... Thus, justice is not lessened by the injustice of others; on the contrary, it proves itself by being tested ... through the virtue of patience. Likewise benevolence and kindness in time of discord are shown in sweet patience; and against envy, displeasure and hatred, loving charity appears in hungry desire for the salvation of souls.

However it is not just a matter of appearance: virtue, thus proved, will act on its adversaries and win them:

I tell you that it is not just a matter of testing virtue in those who return good for bad: I tell you that often they will be throwing [on them] live coals, burning with the fire of charity, which will melt away hatred and resentment from angry hearts and make them turn from hatred to kindness, thanks to the power of love and perfect patience. If you consider the virtue of persevering fortitude, you will see it tested by much suffering, by injuries and slander from people who, by either offence or allurement, might

47

be trying to prevent our going along the way of true doctrine. . . . And if when tested by many opposites it were to fail, it would prove not to be truly founded. (D, VIII)

To give virtue a sound foundation personal effort is necessary. In advising her Florentine friends, Francesco di Pipino and his wife Agnes, Catherine is rather exacting:

I want you, my sweet children, thoroughly to attend to killing the perverse sensual will, always trying to rebel against God. And this is how to kill it: mount to the chair of your conscience and pass judgement on yourselves, never allowing the slightest thought opposed to God to pass without redressing it by hard reproach. Make a clear distinction between sensuality and reason, and make reason unsheathe the double-edged sword, hatred of vice and love of virtue, using it to make a servant of sensuality by uprooting and throwing away from the soul any vice or vicious bent. Refuse to give that servant whatever she may ask, but trample her under the feet of affection by love of virtue. Suppose she wants to sleep, you on your part insist on vigil and humble prayer; should she turn to lust, you should resort to chastisement; were she to rest in idleness, you should apply yourselves to your work . . . Master yourselves, but always with discernment, giving the body what it needs with regard to bodily life according to natural requirements, so that the body may be a fit instrument in aiding the soul to exert itself for God's sake. (L, 265)

This sounds rather stern but in giving advice Catherine is always mindful whom she is addressing, as can be seen in comparing the letter to Francesco di Pipino with one to Sister Daniella, who seems to have had a peculiar attachment to penitential practices: no, says Catherine, this is not in tune with the rule of discernment:

When the body is feeble, or sick, . . . one must not only cease fasting: he must eat meat, and if once a day is not enough, let him have it four times. If he cannot lie on the floor, let him do so on his bed; if he cannot kneel, let him sit or lie down. This is what discernment requires. (L, 213)

Of all human qualities, discernment is one of Catherine's most cherished. It is a shoot sprouting from the tree of love, the human soul. It is a light on our path preventing our going astray from it. It rules charity itself by showing how to order our actions according to a scale of values, so that our activity and wealth can be given for the welfare of others; our bodily life is well spent for the salvation of souls, but our soul is never to be sacrificed, because nothing but sin could destroy it, and to offend God is the worst of all evils.[8] When the eye of discernment is wide open we can avoid paying undue attention to what is of only secondary importance, and mistaking the instrument for the goal, as happens when too much stress is put on bodily penance. God is not to be pleased with acts which are necessarily limited; what he wants is the homage of our free will, infinite desire. If we thought that spiritual progress could be identified with physical penance we would be deceived: excessive attachment to such exercises would only feed our self-esteem and make us despise those who do not follow in our wake or refuse to be moulded in our own mould. Such people, says Catherine, a little wry smile on her lips, pretend to rule the Holy Spirit.

The infinite variety in the ways God can open to human souls should be a cause of rejoicing and wonder if seen in its true light, revealing the surprising endless resources of the Creator's inventiveness. Within the one way to the Father, which is Christ, each man or woman has his own path corresponding to a providential design. As we admire the beauty of nature in the almost infinite variety of creation, we should admire the variety in the world of the spirit and find in it a reason for praise:

> Those who stay in this sweet light . . . are always enjoying peace and rest and are never scandalized, because they have renounced their own will, the cause of scandal. Persecutions from the world or the devil flow under their feet: they stay in the waters of many hardships and temptations with no damage, because they cling to the branch of burning desire. They rejoice in everything, and do not pass judgement on my servants or on any reasonable creature; rather, they rejoice in the various situations and ways they come to know and say: 'Thanks be given to you, eternal Father, for the many mansions in your house.' And they are made happier by seeing such diversity than if they had seen everyone going along the same way, because they can better come to know how large the extent of my goodness is. In everything they rejoice and find the fragrance of the rose. (D, C)

The sweet pure rose is God's eternal will creating us in love, and returning us to life 'in that most ardent red rose, the blood of Christ',[9] giving us assurance that his never-failing love will always be leading us to the house of the Father, there to see, unveiled, the perfect Model that we portray.

Notes

1. No. 8; P, XXII.
2. P, I. This passage can be illuminated by Augustine, *De Trinitate*, XIV, 12: 'Then this trinity of the spirit is not an image of God inasmuch as the spirit remembers itself, understands and loves itself; but because it can also remember, understand and love him by whom it was created. When it does so, it is made wise.'
3. Cf. Sirach 15:17: 'In front of man stand life and death, good and evil: what he chooses shall be given to him.'
4. Cf. 1 Peter 1:18–19.
5. In this passage, an evident reminiscence of Psalm 8, particular stress is laid on the additional beauty that the living presence of fish and birds lends to sea and sky, which might imply that beauty is another need of human nature for which its Creator kindly provides.
6. The Jerusalem Bible reads: 'Where two or three meet in my name, I shall be there *with* them', but Catherine must have had in mind the Latin text of the Vulgate, 'ibi sum *in medio* eorum', or a similar Italian version.
7. Catherine may have been referring to Romans 12:12–13: 'keep on praying. If any of the saints are in need, you must share with them'; but, because she quotes from memory, the passages she refers to are often difficult to identify. This is particularly true when she quotes St Paul, because, we may speculate, of her familiarity with him.
8. Cf. L, 213.
9. Cf. L, 362.

4

The imagery of the 'tree'

Know that your soul is a tree
made out of love
and this is why it cannot live
on anything but love. (D, X)

In the rich imagery that Catherine uses to lend her words the
immediacy of vision, the image of a tree is among her favourites.
This image recurs more than once in her writings and is developed
according to its various facets. In the *Dialogue*, after being taught
about virtues and vices and how neither can be practised except in
relations with neighbours, she is asked to consider the human soul
as 'a tree of love':

Suppose you had a round circle laid down on the soil, and a tree
sprouting from its middle with a young shoot alongside. The tree
draws its nourishment from the soil within the circle; were it to
be outside the soil, it would wither and yield no fruit until it was
planted again in the soil. Think, then, that the soul is a tree made
out of love, and therefore it cannot live on anything except love.
(D, X)

The allegory is then explained: the circle having neither beginning
nor ending is a symbol of the twofold knowledge which our soul
should make its constant abode; the soil within the circle stands for
humility, which means truth, since 'true humility comes from
knowledge of self'. Therefore, the wider the circle of knowledge,
the larger the soil of humility.[1] Humility founded on true knowledge fosters charity; it is its wet-nurse, according to Catherine, and

the tree of love draws its sap from the fertile soil of humility. Patience, the heart of the tree, is a sure sign of the presence of charity in the soul, implying God's presence.

> This tree, so gently planted, produces sweet-scented flowers of many different savours; it yields the fruit of grace to the soul and fruit of help to neighbours, according to their willingness to accept the fruit of my servants. To me it renders the fragrance of glory and praise to my name, thus achieving my aim in creating it. (D, X)

A young sprout shoots forth from the trunk and grows alongside the tree: it stands for discernment, the output of humility and love, and it seasons all the fruit of the tree, thus leading the soul to its perfection.

Can a tree firmly rooted in the soil give an idea of so subtle a reality as the human soul? It seems so, since there is an ancient and venerable tradition in which trees stand as symbols of man and his behaviour. We read in Holy Scripture that observance of the Law makes a man

> like a tree that is planted by water streams, yielding its fruit in season, its leaves never fading. (Ps 1:3)

And Jeremiah is even more optimistic: the man who puts his trust in Yahweh

> is like a tree by the waterside that thrusts its roots to the stream: when the heat comes it feels no alarm, its foliage stays green; it has no worries in a year of drought, and never ceases to bear fruit. (Jer 17:8)

At the very dawn of mankind, in the beautiful garden of Eden, we find a tree already bearing signs of contradiction, and Matthew's Gospel stresses the fact that all trees are not necessarily patterns of beauty and goodness: by their fruit we are told what they are:

> Can people pick grapes from thorns or figs from thistles? In the same way a sound tree produces good fruit, but a rotten tree bad fruit. (Matt 7:16–17)

Fruits, then, reveal not only the genus of a tree, but also its being sound or rotten. This means that a good tree may turn bad, just as the soul, which is created good, can lose its innate righteousness, and also recover it, as is hinted in the parable of the fig tree that had been barren for three years: the farmer wanted to have it cut down, but the labourer entreated him on its behalf: he would till the ground, spread manure and maybe next year it would bear fruit.[2] A fruit tree *has* to yield fruit, and the 'tree of love' must yield the 'fruit of grace to the soul and fruit of help to neighbours' because to give help is an act of love increasing the merit of the giver.

In a letter to Countess Benedicta, a member of the Salimbeni family, Catherine develops the figure of the soul as a tree and explains how its growth should be fostered. Her desire regarding Benedicta is to see her 'founded on true and perfect charity', which calls for an explanation about this virtue:

> What is charity? It is love ineffable, which the soul draws from its Creator by its whole affection and might. I said the soul draws it from its Creator, and so it is; but how? By love, since love cannot be acquired except by love and from love.

Love must have an object, and the object must be known, and to know it we need light. God provides for the need of the soul by giving it understanding, its noblest part: an eye whose pupil is most holy faith.

> The soul cannot live without loving, nor could it love without light. Then, if it wants to love, it has to see.

Light is necessary not only to see what to love, but also to avoid loving what is not worth loving, and this is where faith comes to help the natural discernment of reason:

> Nothing can be loved or seen apart from God without its turning deadly to us. This is why what we love we must love in him and for his sake, by acknowledging that we owe our own being and everything to his goodness. You understand, then, that this is how one loves and sees, because without loving and without seeing there is no life.

Then, for a better understanding of the care one should have of the soul, Catherine introduces the image of the tree:

> Do you not see, dearest child, that we are a tree of love, having been made out of love? This tree is so well planted that nobody can prevent its growing or yielding fruit unless it consents. Besides, God has given this tree a labourer to till it, because he likes it, and the labourer is free will. Should it not have this labourer, the soul would not be free and, not being free, could be

excused when it sins; but it can have no excuse since nothing, neither the world nor the devil nor the frailty of flesh, can compel it to any sin unless it is willing to consent. This tree, in fact, has reason in itself, provided free will makes use of it; it has the eye of the understanding, recognizing the truth it sees when the fog of self-love does not dim its sight. In this light one sees where the tree has to be planted, because if one did not see nor have this sweet power of the mind, the labourer might excuse himself by saying: I was free, but did not see where I could plant my tree, either on high or low down. But this he cannot say since he has a mind that sees, and reason, a tie of rational love, which can bind it, and engraft it to the tree of life, Christ the sweet Jesus.

Once it has been planted in the fertile soil of humility within the enclosed garden – a substitute for the double circle of knowledge of God and of self – the tree grows so tall that no human eye can reach and see where its top unites with infinite Godhead. As the tree in the fenced garden, so must the soul stay in the cell of the twofold knowledge, persisting in contemplating Christ crucified: he is the very source of love because through him we come to know God's boundless love.

Here Catherine adds an important statement to her former answer to the question: how can love be drawn? Her answer had been: by love and from love. Now, after defining the meaning of 'from love', she stresses 'by love' and uses a new image, that of the sponge. A sponge is naturally disposed to absorb water; likewise, our heart is naturally ready to fill itself with love. But, just as the sponge needs a hand to plunge it in water, so does the soul need something to put it into contact with the source of love. That 'something' is free will, acting in the light of reason. Thus Catherine stresses the voluntary nature of the act of love which is anything but passive: it is the result of the encounter of reason and will freely joining in turning into action the soul's innate disposition to love.

When the heart – now turned from sponge to basin – has been filled with the water of love, it has to pour it out for the benefit of others. But, since whatever we do on behalf of neighbours turns to our own profit, the watering of the soil fosters the growth of the tree either directly or in the shape of dew and rain. Why dew and why rain? We can conjecture that dew may be understood as the gentle action of mental prayer, where virtues are conceived, while the heavy rain washing the leaves and refreshing the fruit can stand for the impact of people, anything but gentle at times, but of vital importance for virtues to become 'true and real', as Catherine wants them to be, in confrontation with their opposites. When so well-tilled and nourished, the tree stretches its branches wide and yields such fruits as prayer, examples of honest life or, whenever possible, material help, while it offers the flowers of honour to God, to whom they belong. The same flowers, blooming out of charity, will become fruits: the fruit of virtues whose mother is charity.

To impress Benedicta further with the importance of true love, Catherine presents new images to her attention: charity is a sweet queen worth our fighting for like brave knights; it is the nuptial robe giving access to the eternal wedding banquet, so precious that one should be careful to get and keep it at any cost. But Catherine returns to the image of the tree and with it closes the letter:

> I beg you, for the sake of Christ crucified, to do your best in making this foundation . . . and you will not have to be afraid of contrary winds . . . But, since winds cannot injure the tree in the valley, have a humble and kind heart. (L, 113)

The letter to Countess Benedicta is supposed to have been written in the spring of 1377; a few months later Catherine was to be the guest of the Salimbeni at Rocca d'Orcia. Was it the land-scape from the top of the hill, or her dealing with its proud lords, that suggested the counterpart of the tree of love?

> There is a tree that produces nothing but deadly fruit, putrid flowers, stained leaves, branches bent down to the ground, shattered by various winds. (D, XCIII)

A description of the tree of death is given in the *Dialogue* within the 'Doctrine on Tears', where distinction is made between tears of life and tears of death,

> the tears of the wicked, worldly people: they are tears of damnation. (D, LXXXVIII)

Tears are the output of the heart and their being good or bad depends on the disposition of their source:

> I want you to understand – says the Lord – that all tears spring from the heart, since of all parts of the body none is so ready to comply with the heart as the eye. If one is suffering, the eye will show it, and if suffering is caused by sensual love, the heartfelt tears it pours are deadly because of their coming from a heart whose love is unruly. (D, LXXXIX)[3]

Catherine is first told about life-giving tears in their fourfold division, corresponding to the steps of the bridge leading to its fourth stage; then she is taught about deadly tears as depicted in the bad tree:

> A virtuous soul sets the roots of its tree in the valley of true humility, but the miserable wicked have placed them on the mountain of pride. (D, XCIII)

Having been planted in the wrong place, this tree cannot be expected to produce life-giving fruits: it has to yield deadly ones, together with stinking flowers, the heart's wicked feelings: hatred of neighbours and love of self, with a distorted valuation of God's doings and of the behaviour of people.

> The fruits are their doings, all poisoned by many, varied sins ...
> I said that the flowers are putrid, and so they are. Such flowers are the heart's stinking feelings that I dislike: hatred and displeasure of neighbours. Like thieves, they steal honour from me and give it to themselves. (Ibid.)

The stench of these flowers is the misunderstanding of God's mysterious ways and of the behaviour of others:

> A miserable man who does not even know himself will pretend that he knows the heart and feelings of another person and, by one action he may happen to have seen or words heard, will pretend to pass judgement on the dispositions of somebody's heart ...
>
> Leaves come next: words poured out of the mouth in scorn of me and of the blood of my only-begotten Son, and to the injury of neighbours. Their only concern is to curse and criticize all my doings, and to slander every rational creature after their own point of view. ...
>
> Such are the stained leaves of miserable sin, because the heart where they were bred was not sincere; it was, rather, stained with duplicity and misery.
>
> What temporal danger this implies, apart from the spiritual damage in the loss of grace! You have seen and heard about changes in states, ruin of cities and many more evils and murders, because words entered the very heart of the listener; entered as deep as no knife could have reached. (Ibid.)

The branches of this disgraceful tree do not tend upwards; they are bent down, because the soul has no aim except earthly ones:

> I say that the tree has seven branches bending down to the ground from which flowers and leaves sprout out, as I already told you. They are the seven deadly sins, which include many varied sins bound to the root of love of self and pride, that has produced first the branches and the flowers of many intentions; then follow the leaves of words and the fruit of evil doings. They are bent down to the ground because deadly sins are always turned to the earth of frail and disorderly worldly pleasures with no other aim than to feed on earth, insatiably, and are never satiated. Insatiable they are and unbearable to themselves, and it is right they should always be restless since they desire and seek what causes dissatisfaction . . . Man has been placed above all creatures, and no creature is above him. Above him there is nothing except me, God eternal, and therefore only I can satisfy him. And when sin deprives him of me, he stays in continuous torment and pain. Upon pain, tears follow; then come winds and, as winds come, they shake the tree sprouted out of sensuality. (Ibid.)

Such tears might still be tears of death, but God contrives to turn them into tears of life by causing four winds to blow against the tree. Their names are prosperity, adversity, fear and conscience.

First comes prosperity. It is not bad in itself, even though it might foster pride, but it is meant to increase dissatisfaction with earthly advantages and turn the soul to worthier aims.

Next comes the wind of slavish fear. It makes a person afraid of losing his possessions or privileges and prevents his enjoying them in peace, to the point that his own shadow frightens him.

While the wind of fear is still shaking the tree, adversity blows away what one has cherished, such as relatives, health, authority, prestige, wealth, according to what the supreme Physician chooses as a fit remedy to restore sanity. But the results of the treatment might be negative if rebellion and impatience were to ensue. If the heart has not changed its disposition, the eye would still weep tears of death.

The fourth and last wind is conscience. It calls to repentance and sincere conversion, but some will avoid its spur, being too strongly attached to their miserable pleasures. Such trees are so putrid that they turn to death what is offered to give them life; they stay in unceasing pain and complaint, which will turn to eternal mourning unless they repent during their life-time.[4] God is so fond of man, and of his own plan for man's welfare, that he is unwilling to give up and invents all sorts of contrivances to make man turn from death to life, but will never impose on his free will. If man comes to understand why the winds are blowing, and allows them to do what they are sent for, then his eye will weep tears of life.

A different description of the trees of death is given in another part of the *Dialogue*, after the presentation of the tree of love and of the bridge which the Word incarnate made of himself, building together the solid virtues he practised in his lifetime. These trees stand for whoever, being too strongly attached to bad habits, refuses to go along the way of the bridge. Four are described, each one embodying a particular vice, the vices most harmful to the soul. They make it insensible to the warnings of conscience, the little worm gnawing inside, whose gentle appeals are overcome by a boisterous love of self.

> The fruit of this tree is mortal: sap having been drawn by the root of pride, the miserable soul is full of ingratitude, whence all evils proceed. Were it grateful for the bounty it has been granted, it would come to know me, and in knowing me it would know itself and stay in my love; but in its blindness it will reach for some hold in the river, and does not see that the water will not stay and wait for it. (D, XXXI)

Ingratitude or indifference to the gift of redemption leads the soul to prefer the swollen river to the safe way of the bridge. These trees, by contrast to the tree of love, have impatience for marrow, and lack of understanding or stupidity as a side shoot. They yield several kinds of fruit, all deadly.

First comes the vice of impurity. More than any other sin, it deprives man of his dignity; it dims the light of his mind and lowers him to the bestial level: he is made loathsome even to the devil![5]

The second tree personifies avarice:

> Others there are, whose fruit is earth. Such are the greedy misers who behave like the mole, feeding on nothing but earth until they die, and when death comes there is no remedy for them.

Their companions are the 'cruel usurers' who 'sell time to their neighbours', have no regard for the very members of their own families and, provided they get money, would not refrain from crime.

Alas; how many evils come from this confounded sin! How many murders, thefts, plunders together with unlawful profits, and hard-hearted cruelty and injustice to neighbours! It kills the soul and enslaves it to riches, makes it unmindful of God's commandments. Such a man does not love anybody, except to his own advantage. (D, XXXIII)

Avarice is a product of and a stimulus to pride. And in pride are the third and fourth trees rooted. Catherine's sketch of the proud petty lord is not without humour:

Others there are who keep their heads upright, because they have some power, and bear the banner of injustice, which means that they do not pay their debts, of honour and gratitude to God, of help to neighbours, of virtue to themselves, having been blinded by love of self. (D, XXXIV)

Such love can easily lead to false judgement about God's doings and the behaviour of people. And this is the fourth tree of death.

Since the heart is rotten and the taste is corrupt, good is sensed as bad, and bad as good. (D, XXXV)

Catherine closes her review of the bad trees with a complaint against human voluntary blindness, forgetful of human dignity, and a reminder of the opportunity for rescue: the blood of Christ that has earned for all human beings victory over vice.

God is constantly recalling men and women through his disciples, by the example of righteous life, and will not fail to help those who try to come out of the river and turn to the bridge, while a harder final reproach can be expected at the point of death by those who stay in the 'dead water' of sin:

Get up, you who are dead to grace, and being dead [in your souls] come to bodily death; get up and come before the supreme Judge with your injustice and false judgement, the lamp of your faith extinguished. You had that lamp lit in holy baptism, and you blew it out with the wind of your heart's pride and vanity, which you displayed like a sail to the winds opposed to your welfare; you fostered the wind of your reputation and the sail of self-love, so that you hastened along the river of worldly pleasures and great status after your own whim, being led by the frailty of flesh and the devil's worries and temptations. And by the sail of your own will has the devil drawn you along the way underneath, the flowing river, leading you to share his eternal damnation. (D, XXXVI)

Even at the point of death man is offered the possibility of repenting and being saved, provided he does not despair of God's mercy. Despair is the worst of all sins; it is the extreme output of evil judgement and self-estimation, giving more weight to one's faults than to God's infinite mercy:

> This is the sin that is never forgiven, my mercy having been spurned in its being refused . . . I was more displeased by Judas's despair, and it weighed heavier on my Son than his very treason. (Ibid.)

Catherine's way of surveying the torments of the damned appears rather singular, and the more so if compared with contemporary paintings, clearly influenced by Dante's *Inferno*, describing a variety of punishments, such as fire, mud, restless motion or immobility, biting snakes and cutting blades, corresponding precisely to the character of each sin; a very clever contrivance, no doubt, to impress the sinner with the deceptive results of the delight one was looking for in sinning. But how can bodily torments have an impact on beings deprived of body? Catherine's solution reflects her love of truth and is faithful to the Gospel and to Church teaching: since eternal bliss is essentially the vision of Godhead, the essential cause of sorrow cannot but be our being deprived of it. Moreover, all sins have a common source in the side shoot of the bad tree: lack of discernment is the cause of all misbehaviour, just as discernment seasons all good doings. In speaking of the condition of the damned, Catherine insists on such words as 'to see', 'sight', 'vision':

> The first [torment] is their seeing themselves deprived of my vision, and this is so piercing that, could they choose, they would rather stay in fire and torments and see me, than be away from chastisement without seeing me.
>
> This suffering is made more painful by the worm of conscience which is always gnawing as they see that they are being deprived of me and of intercourse with the angels through their own fault, which has made them deserve association with demons and being given the vision of them.
>
> This sight of the devil, their third torment, redoubles labour. Therefore, as in the vision of me the blessed exult in a joyful renewal of the fruit of the labours they so lovingly endured for my sake with self-denial, so have these miserable ones their

torments renewed in the vision of the devils, because by their sight they come to a better knowledge of themselves, which is to say that by their own fault they have earned such doom. And so the worm gnaws more and more, and the fire of such awareness burns ceaselessly. All that is made more painful by their seeing the devil in its proper shape, so horrid that no human heart could imagine it . . .

The fourth torment is fire. Such fire blazes without burning out because the soul cannot be destroyed; it is not a material thing to be burnt out by fire, it is incorporeal. But my divine justice adapted fire to give them the tormenting pain of burning so that it should torment without consuming; it tortures and scorches them piercingly in different ways and degrees according to the various sins, and the greater or lesser culpability of the sinner.

From these four torments come all the others, with cold and heat and grinding of teeth. (D, XXXVIII)[6]

In the absence of love, their dismal dwelling, the doomed are afflicted by a fifth sight: the happiness of the blessed. Such sight adds bitterness to their feelings as it makes them aware of what they have lost through their own fault, while for the citizens of the City of Love to see one another's bliss makes a renewal of rejoicing.

In love, they enjoy the eternal vision of me, having been enabled to share my own good, each one according to his measure, which is to say that by the measure of love they had when they came to me will they be measured. Having dwelt in my love and in that of their neighbours, and being united by general and specific charity, both coming from the same source, they rejoice and exult in sharing one another's good under the impulse of charity, in addition to the universal good all of them enjoy. . . . All are bound by the binding of charity, but more closely so with those they were more closely bound to in life. . . .

When one soul enters eternal life, all partake in the good of that soul, and the soul in theirs. . . . They see that by my mercy it has been taken from earth in the plenitude of grace, and therefore they exult in me because of the favour that soul has been granted. And the soul rejoices in me and in the blessed and in the angels in seeing and savouring in them the sweetness of my love. Their desires are ever appealing to me for the salvation of the whole world . . . You see, then, that within the binding of love which was binding them when their lives came to an end, they are still bound, and it is to last for ever.

Thus love, the law of human nature, will have its fulfilment in happiness while its lack will cause sorrow, both being made sensible to the soul through the mind's eye.

> The desire of the blessed is to see my honour in you, the travellers, the pilgrims hastening to the end of [earthly] life. Within the desire of my honour they desire your salvation, which causes them to pray for you unceasingly. Their desire is fulfilled unless you are so ignorant as to refuse my mercy. (D, XLI)

Future life is thus presented in the opposite perspectives of love and hatred and stress is laid once more on responsible choice:

> Nobody has ever to be afraid of any fight or temptation . . . because I have made them strong, and gifted them with the stronghold of will, that my Son's blood has further strengthened. Neither devil nor any creature can shake it: it is your own as I gave it to you together with free choice. You can keep or let it go as you choose. It is a weapon: when you put it in the devil's hands it is a knife that can wound and slay you. But as long as one does not place this knife, his own will, in the devil's hands by consenting to temptations and troubles, he shall never be offended by sinful culpability; the struggle will rather make him stronger, provided he opens his mind's eye to see that my charity suffers you to be tempted so that you may acquire virtues and bring them to the test.
>
> See, then, man's foolishness in making himself feeble, whom I made strong, and in surrendering to the devil even to the point of grafting himself to the 'dead tree' he is. (D, XLIII; L, 27)

Desire of pleasure and fear of suffering form the devil's bait to catch man and drive him to evil doing; a bait he can skilfully vary depending on whom he wants to bite it, layman or religious, churchman or secular lord:

> By the hook of pleasure he catches them under appearance of profit. In fact he could not do so in any other way because they would never allow themselves to be caught unless they expected to gain some advantage or pleasure, since the human soul, according to its nature, is always seeking for good. But the soul that has been blinded by love of self does not know which good is the real one. (D, XLIV)

To make her understand how important it is to discern real good and, as such, worth striving for even at the cost of suffering,

Catherine is reminded, in the *Dialogue*, of another tree she was once shown, not as an image of the human soul, but of Christ himself, the model of human perfection and goal of perfect enjoyment.

You know – says the Lord – that I then showed myself to you in the shape of a tree, of which you could see neither beginning nor ending, but you saw that it was rooted in the ground, depicting my divine nature united to the earth of your humanity. At the foot of the tree, as you may remember, there were some thorns, from which all the lovers of their own sensuality recoiled, and rushed to a heap of husk, which I meant you to understand as an image of all worldly pleasures. The husk looked like wheat, but was not, and therefore, as you saw, many who stayed within it starved to death while others, having come to know the trick of the world, went back to the tree through the thorns by voluntary determination. Which deliberation, before it is made, feels like a thorn bush in the way of truth. Conscience from one side and sensuality from the other are always struggling. But once, through hatred and displeasure of self, someone takes his manly stand and says: 'I will follow Christ crucified', he immediately breaks the thorns and finds inestimable sweetness . . .

You know that I then told you: 'I am your immovable God and I do not move away. I do not avoid any creature that wants to come to me.'

I have shown them the truth by making myself visible, I, the invisible; I have shown what it is to love anything without me. But they, being blinded by the cloud of disordered love, do not know either me or themselves. See how deceived they are: they would rather starve to death than go through a few thorns. (Ibid.)

The beautiful tall tree, Christ God-and-man, is continually offering its life-giving fruit beyond the thorn hedge which we should not allow to prevent us from reaching it. Suffering cannot be avoided in any case in earthly life, but love can turn it into pleasure. Catherine had been told that the more someone conforms to Christ in suffering the greater share will he have in his glory, and was advised to make bitterness taste sweet, and sweetness bitter. The fragrance of the rose comes from a bush of thorns.[7]

To rescue ignorant man and make him aware of his worth, eternal Wisdom grafted himself onto the old, withering tree of humankind and gave it new life.

O eternal Godhead, what a wonderful sight it is to see in your light the pure tree of your creature ... which you united to a body made out of earth! You made it free, you gave it three branches, the powers of the soul, memory, understanding and will ... But, having parted from innocence because of dis-obedience, the tree fell, and from a tree of life it turned to a tree of death. . . . You, high eternal Father ... gave it the cure with the same love you had in creating it, by grafting your Godhead onto the withered tree of humankind. (P, X)

The grafting of the Word of God onto humankind was the first step towards its redemption: Christ, God-and-man, would then graft himself onto the tree of the cross.

O you, pleasant graft, Word incarnate, Son of God! You drew out the worm, Adam's old sin, and took the wild, sour fruit away! In fact, because of sin, our orchard had grown so wild that it could produce no life-giving fruit of virtue. Love, you sweet fire! You have so grafted and bound God to man and man to God that the unfruitful fire causing our death is turned good and fruitful; it always gives us life, provided we make use of our reason. Think of God's ineffable love for you, and consider the sweetness of the fragrant fruit, the immaculate Lamb, the sweet seed, sown in Mary's gentle field! (L, 138)

By consuming his sacrifice on the wood of the cross, the immaculate Lamb has turned that tree, in itself an awful instrument of death, into a source of life, a sure help along our way:

I beg you, then, make your affection and desire rise, and take the tree of the most holy cross, and plant it in the orchard of your soul, laden with the fruit of true and real virtues. Well can you see, in fact, that, besides uniting with his creature, God has reached to the tree of holy cross, and wants, and asks us to unite on that tree through love and desire; then will our orchard yield no fruit except sweet and fragrant ones. (Ibid.)

In considering the cross, Catherine's genius for imagery finds a most fertile field. The cross is the table on which the Lamb, 'roasted' on the spit of the cross by the fire of his burning love, is offered as food to our souls; it is a sure support against the devil's efforts to make us fall; it is the horse on whose back Christ fought his victorious battle, and the banner that will lead us to victory; it is the mast displaying the sail of charity to the wind of holy desire, of the boat itself, our soul, safely sailing on a troubled sea to a safe haven.[8] The soul that sets the tree of the cross at the very core of itself is made a garden fragrant with many flowers, the flowers of holy desires. There

> on the tree of most holy cross rests the immaculate Lamb; he pours streams of blood that moisten and flood the sweet and glorious garden, and holds the ripe fruit of true, genuine virtues. (L, 241)

The silent suffering of the Lamb proclaims his deeply rooted, mild patience; his humility is shown in his submitting to the human condition and to shameful death. It all comes from his charity: love kept him nailed to the cross: iron nails and wood could not have held him, God-and-man: the power of his charity did. Thus the tree of the cross, by its contact with the holy body of Christ, becomes a fit instrument to help the soul develop into a perfect tree of love.

> No wonder if the soul, that through knowledge has made a garden of itself, is so strong as to stand against the whole world since it has conformed and united itself to supreme fortitude. It begins to enjoy a foretaste of eternal life while still in earthly life; it sways the world by despising it. Devils do not dare to approach a soul all afire with divine charity. (Ibid.)

To kindle divine fire in the human soul Christ caused himself to be lifted up on the tree of the cross, so that the sight of his sacrifice should make God's love for humankind clearly known, and draw to him the hearts of men and women, since man's heart is ever drawn by love. And once the soul has attained perfect love, its vital need appeased, it can rest and rejoice. Then the tree of the cross becomes the ideal place to stay and rest away from trouble, as hinted in the closing greetings in one of Catherine's letters:

> Stay in God's holy and sweet love, ever resting on the branches of the genuine tree, most holy cross. (L, 137)

The cross stretches its strong arms wide for us to stay and rest, like little birds perched on high branches that need not worry if big dogs are barking at them. But to enjoy rest on that tree, we must have risen above ourselves, which is to say, above selfish love, to the highest level of perfect love, where Christ crucified is inviting us to reach and receive his kiss of peace. There, in its full union with God's will, shall our soul be a true image of that 'tree of love' which First Love conceived in calling it to life.

Notes

1. Catherine could have no difficulty, Latin being still very much alive in her time, in relating *humility* to *humus*, soil.
2. Cf. Luke 13:6–9.
3. Cf. Matthew 15:18–19: 'the things that come out of the mouth come from the heart, and it is these that make a man unclean. For from the heart come evil intentions: murder, adultery, fornication, theft, perjury, slander'; and Mark 7:22 adds to the list 'avarice, malice, deceit, indecency, envy, pride, folly'. The connection between heart and eye, as well as the discerning capacity of the eye, recalls another passage in the Gospels: Matthew 6:22–23: 'The lamp of the body is the eye. It follows that if your eye is sound, your whole body will be filled with light. But if your eye is diseased, your whole body will be all darkness.'
4. Cf. D, XCIV.
5. Cf. D, XXXII.
6. 'Grinding of teeth' recurs more than once in Matthew as applied to the damned. In Luke 13:28 it is associated with the pain of seeing: 'when you see Abraham and Isaac and Jacob and all the prophets in the kingdom of God, and yourselves turned outside'.
7. Cf. *Life*, 104; L, 137.
8. Italian has one word, *albero*, for both 'tree' and 'mast'. And Catherine's *arbore* is an unmistakable offshoot of the Latin *arbor*; cf. L, 159. As regards the other images, the 'dining table' recurs too frequently to be quoted – more than 40 times – while 'spit' is to be found once, L, 52. For the cross as 'support', cf. L, 60 and for 'horse', L, 112, 156, 260; 'banner' can be found 39 times.

5

Catherine's Christology

Life to me is Christ. (Phil 1:21)

On the feast of the Conversion of St Paul, 25 January 1377, Catherine was praying:

> You, excellent Paul, ... having been converted by the Word from error to truth, after you had been granted to be caught up to paradise where you saw the divine essence in three persons, you were deprived of such sight, and wrapped yourself in the exclusive vision of the Word incarnate. And, as you attentively considered that the same incarnate Word attained the Father's honour and our own salvation through continuous pain, you were made thirsty for suffering so that, unmindful of anything else, you might proclaim that you knew nothing but Christ, and Christ crucified. (P, XXIII)

Catherine, so close in spirit to the great apostle as to call him with the familiar diminutive 'Paoluccio', might well have borrowed his words in claiming the constant, fundamental presence of Christ crucified in her own doctrine: Christ carrying from the very beginning of his human existence the cross of desire to fulfil the obedience imposed on him by the Father; Christ, the lover and rescuer of mankind, making of his life a model for us to imitate through the practice of charity, the mother of virtues; the paschal Lamb nailed to the cross and given us every day as food in the Eucharist.

Even a cursory reading of the *Dialogue* can show the primary relevance of Christ and his doctrine in Catherine's thought: his presence marks both the opening and the solemn conclusion of the book, and the book is centred on the teaching of Christ-the-bridge. Catherine normally begins her letters 'in the name of Christ crucified' and closes them in that of 'sweet Jesus'. Her Christology can be understood as a commentary of the account he gave of himself, which she quotes more than once: 'He said: "I am the way and truth and life"' (D, XXVII).[1]

'Sweet first Truth', Catherine's favoured substitute for the name of God, is rightly applied to Christ, true God and true man or, as she puts it, 'all God and all man'. He is the eternal Word of the Father, eternally expressing the ineffable truth of the Godhead; he is the Word incarnate making the same eternal Truth audible to human ears through the vibrations of a human voice. He is the visible image of the Father:

> I, the invisible, made myself visible as it were in the Word, my only-begotten Son. (D, LXII)

Or, as Christ himself said to Philip: 'who sees me, sees the Father' (John 14:9).

When speaking to Catherine, the Father will often call him 'my Truth':

> as my Truth said in holy Gospel . . . (D, CXXI)

but 'my truth' may also mean God's loving plan for man's happy destiny, to which Christ's life and death bear witness; a plan that the devil, 'the father of falsehood', tries to hinder and 'God's Truth' restores:

> This truth is that I had created him in my image and likeness that he should have eternal life, and share and savour my supreme sweetness and bounty. Because of his sin he could not reach the goal, which prevented my truth from having its fulfilment. (D, XXI)

Redemption is seen by Catherine as the victory of truth over falsehood. A deceptive promise of greatness, 'you will be like gods' (Gen 3:5), fostered rebellion and disobedience; Christ's obedient humiliation opens to man the way of love to union with God in union of will:

> look at those who are clad in the nuptial vestment of charity adorned with many true virtues: they are united to me by love.

> Therefore I tell you that if you were to ask me who they are, I would say . . . they are another myself, because they have lost and drowned their own will, and have clothed and united and conformed themselves with mine. (D, I)

Because of her sense of humour Catherine may have enjoyed the idea of truth making use of deceit to overcome the great deceiver who was not aware of the Godhead hidden within Christ's humanity: he thought he could destroy the man and was overcome by his divinity, like a little fish biting the bait and being caught by the hook inside (D, CXXXV).

In fact, during his very normal life, Christ's divine nature could scarcely be known; it was like live coals under cinders, but the flame of almighty Love burnt bright when he came to his passion. Then the love of the Father offering his own Son for the rescue of humankind could not be mistaken, nor could the love of the Word incarnate who was undergoing such hard suffering in obedience to the Father for our sake. Catherine even feels that having had to stay 'under cinders' throughout his life must have been a harder strain than bodily sufferings and death. On recalling Christ's words at the Last Supper, 'I have longed to eat this passover with you before I suffer' (Luke 22:15), Catherine notes that many a time had he eaten passover with his disciples, but this was a particular one because the desire which had been a hard trial for him all through his life was now approaching its fulfilment.[2] She expressed the same thought in prayer, on the feast of the Annunciation:

> O Mary, my sweetest love . . . I see that this Word . . . was never lacking the cross of holy desire; on the contrary, as soon as he was conceived in you he was engrafted with the desire to die for the salvation of man, such being the cause for his incarnation, so that having to bear so long that desire which he would have liked to fulfil at once was indeed a heavy cross. (P, XI)

There is an innate need to know in human beings just because there is as great a need to love, and there can be no love without an object. Catherine has given a very concise expression to this reality:

> Without knowing and without loving we cannot live. (L, 113)

Our mind is uneasy until it reaches absolute truth, so that doubt – says Dante – shoots up at its feet like a young sprout from the trunk, our natural impulse urging us on from height to height.[3]

However, our desire to know when aimed at transcendent reality is made aware of its limits:

> O God eternal, high eternal magnitude, you are great but I am small, so that my lowliness cannot attain to your loftiness, except inasmuch as affection and understanding together with memory rise above my lowly humanity and by the light you give me within your light, come to know you. But if I consider your loftiness, any possible rising of my soul towards you is like dark night in comparison with sunshine, or as moonshine differs from the sphere of the sun.

Yet, such innate desire, prompted by the very nature of man, must be given a response:

> But, when was I enabled to attain the depth of your charity? . . . When it was time, and the sacred time came to its plenitude . . . When the great physician, your only-begotten Son, came to the world, when the bridegroom joined his bride, as the Word's Godhead united with our humanity. . . . Still, such a loving union was so hidden that few were aware of it. But, as I can see in your light, the human soul came to full knowledge of your impelling charity in the Word's passion; then, in fact, the fire hidden under our cinders began to appear large and full through the opening of his most holy body on the wood of the cross. And to draw the soul's affection to higher objects and cause the eye of the mind to gaze into the fire, you, eternal Word, wanted to be raised on high where you could show us love in your blood. (P, XII)[4]

'God's truth', his love of mankind, must be known, since its revelation was the very aim of the Word's incarnation and passion. By being elevated on high he made it visible and attractive to man's mind and heart.

The height of the cross then shifts in Catherine's mind to that of a teacher's chair; we, the little schoolchildren, are to sit down and listen to supreme Wisdom's teaching. He is the teacher and the book; a book that any ignorant illiterate can read, the red heading marks of the paragraphs so evidently recalling the blood of his wounds.[5]

Christ crucified is not only the revealer of God in his 'foolish' love for man; he also reveals to man the mystery of his own dignity, which God deemed worth the sacrifice of his own Son. As Catherine reviews in her mind the material instruments of the crucifixion, she finds them inadequate for the purpose and unable to harm their Creator; nothing but his love for man could have held him nailed to the cross:

> We were the ground where the banner of the holy cross was set, we stayed as a basin to receive the blood of the Lamb that was flowing down the cross. Why were we that ground? Because earth could not have held the cross upright: it had rather refused such injustice; nor was any nail sufficient to keep him fixed and nailed to the cross, unless his ineffable love for our salvation had kept him there. It was, then, his charity towards the honour of the Father and our salvation that kept him [there]. (L, 102)

The great distance between man and other creatures is thus stressed: no created being might have forced God-and-man to cruel death: only love for man, his own brother and the masterpiece of creation, did this.

But, however noble his nature and happy his destiny, man must always remember that he has to keep his treasure in an earthen vessel and that the talents he has been entrusted with must not be hidden in the ground: they have to be increased. Likewise our natural disposition to love has to be raised to perfection. The teaching imparted from the chair of the cross is not abstract. It is matter-of-fact instruction about the way to reach the goal. And the way and the goal is Christ. He is truth, and the way to truth: the true way to 'first sweet Truth'.

Catherine represents that way in the shape of a bridge spanning the deep chasm which severed earth from heaven as a consequence of sin. The Word of God did not just make a bridge: he made a bridge of himself, by assuming human nature in his divine person. This is why he said: 'I am the way.'

The bridge reaches from heaven to earth, and is the way offered to man for him to reach from earth to heaven. Therefore it has to rest on the earth. But such a huge construction could not have been made simply out of earth: humanity alone was unable to build itself so high. Catherine does not indulge in describing particulars of no real consequence, such as shape or colour, but she explains what the bridge is made of: the solid stones of the virtues Christ practised in his lifetime.

> The stones of the virtues are built on him by my power, since there is not a single virtue which has not been tested in him, and by him all are made alive. Therefore, nobody can have any virtue

that gives the life of grace, except from him, by following him and his doctrine closely. He has matured all virtues and set them, like living stones held together with his blood, so that everyone may go speedily and without fear. (D, XXVII)

Virtues were practised even before the incarnation, but they were not joined together by the mortar of charity, and this is why they could not make a bridge from earth to heaven:

Such stones were not built into masonry before the passion of my Son . . . but when they were shaped and laid down on the body of the Word, my sweet Son, he made a construction of them. (Ibid.)

The mortar connecting the stones was the quicklime of his burning divine charity slaked in the blood he shed in his passion and, as we may assume, even though Catherine does not mention it, the earth of his humanity. And the body on which the stones are laid is his doctrine, which he imparted by example rather than by words:

this is the way this glorious bridge made for you. He first acted, and by his actions built the way, teaching his doctrine through example rather than by words. (D, XXIX)

Christ is the way and is the leader:

He told us the way of love and the doctrine of virtue. He showed how we are to love if we want to have life. Therefore we are bound and obliged to follow him: not to follow him along the way of virtue is to persecute him. There are many who are willing to persecute, unwilling to follow him.[6] They want to go before him, not after, and to form a new, different way: to serve God and acquire virtue without labour. But they are deceived: he is the way. (L, 35)

Mercy shelters the bridge from the rain of divine justice. A small storehouse stands on it, where the body and blood of Christ are kept and distributed to passers-by for their comfort on the long way. Past it they reach the door, which is one with the bridge: Christ himself, who said: 'I am the gate of the sheepfold' (John 10:7).

Therefore, if he says that he is the way, he tells the truth, as I already showed you in the figure of a bridge. He says he is the truth, and so it is, because he is one with me, who am supreme truth, and whoever follows him, goes along the way of truth. And he is life, and those who go after this truth are given the life of grace and cannot starve to death because Truth has made himself your food, nor can they plunge in darkness, because he is light and no falsehood is in him, far from it: his truth destroyed the lie the devil had told Eve. That lie broke the way to heaven, and Truth restored it and built it with his blood. (D, XXVII)

God opens the way of the bridge to every man, but will not compel anybody to take it. The way of the bridge is the way of love, and love cannot be compelled: every single person is free to make a choice, either to accept or refuse it. But, since it is the only way to eternal beatitude, which God wants man to enjoy, the bridge is gifted with a very strong attraction: the power of love as shown at its utmost in the passion and death of God's own Son.

The bridge is, in fact, the Word incarnate, Christ crucified. In his staying on high, nailed to the wood of the cross, Catherine sees the fulfilment of his promise: 'When I am lifted on high, I will draw everything to me' (John 12:32).[7]

He drew everything to himself in this way: by showing his ineffable love for you, because man's heart is always drawn by love. Greater love he could not have shown than to give his own life for you. Forcibly, then, is man drawn by love, unless he is so ignorant as to refuse to be drawn. (D, XXVI)

Ignorance in the creature that has been endowed with reason is most blameful: to ignore what should be one's utmost concern is really foolish. But when a soul proves deaf to love's appeals, then fear can be of help. The fear of being swept away by the swollen river and drowned in its muddy waters will cause it to turn to the bridge and begin to move along it.

The bridge has three steps, corresponding to as many parts in the body of Christ crucified and symbolizing the stages in the ascent to perfect love. The first step is formed by the feet nailed to the cross. At this level, love is far from being perfect, because it is still mingled with fear. Such love is qualified as 'servile' because selfish advantages weigh heavy on it: a servant may love his master, but is probably less concerned about his master's welfare than about his own wages: nothing but fear of losing his job will urge him to do his best. Self-concern makes love imperfect.

The steps on the bridge are meant to encourage travellers along the hard way:

O, how wonderful is it to see such consummate love, that of himself, of his own body, he has made stairs to help us up the painful way and lead us to rest! O dearest son, who might doubt that the way may prove hard at first? But once one has got to the feet of affection, of hatred and love, every bitterness turns sweet. The first step in the body of Christ is, then, on his feet. This is the rule that he once gave to one of his servants by saying: 'Get up, daughter, rise above yourself, and come up to me. And to make it easier to ascend I have made stairs for you, being nailed to the cross.' (L, 74)

The ascent from the first to the second step is the hardest part of the way. It implies ascetical effort, the practice of virtues conceived in assiduous prayer and tested in daily contact with neighbours: it could scarcely be done without the spur of ardent desire. Without that, travellers would feel tired and sit down, or even go back: the human soul cannot stand still; it has to move, be it forward or backward.

Besides breeding virtues, persevering prayer made 'in the house of knowledge of God and knowledge of self' opens the mind to deeper knowledge, thus leading the way to the second step: the wound in the side of Christ. Through it we can enter the 'cave' of his chest and be introduced to 'the secret of the heart': the divine love that stays at the root of both creation and redemption. Knowledge of such a secret frees the soul from fear and her love turns from servile to friendly. What makes the difference between a servant and a friend is, in fact, that a servant knows little about his master, while between true friends there can be no secrets. As Jesus said, 'a servant does not know his master's business; I call you friends because I have made known to you everything I have learnt from my Father' (John 15:15).

A true friend has no interest in the personal advantages he might get from friendship: were he to see his friend coming, he would not look at his hands for some kind of present; he would look at his heart, at the affection that moves him to come.[8]

Such love, empty of fear and egoism, is perfect, and perfect love leads to union: the soul who has reached the second step rises without any further effort to the third, there to give and receive from Christ the kiss of peace and share his filial love in perfect union of will with the will of the Father.

On reaching the third step, having been made one with Christ, the loving soul 'takes the function of the mouth', the Word's own office. Such an office is twofold: the mouth speaks, the mouth eats:

> The soul first speaks to me with the tongue that stays in the mouth of holy desire; the tongue, I mean, of holy continuous prayer. This tongue can speak actually [by uttering words] and mentally. It speaks mentally when offering to me sweet loving desires for the salvation of souls; it speaks actually in proclaiming the doctrine of my truth, in admonishing, advising, giving witness [to it] without fear of any harm one might receive from the world, boldly proclaiming it to everybody in different ways according to the variety of situations. (D, LXXVI)

The metaphor of 'eating the food of souls' is fully developed: the mouth of desire has two rows of teeth, hatred of sin and love of virtue; together they crush such obstacles as sneers and insults, reproach and persecution. When the food has been properly chewed and savoured it is swallowed and fills the stomach almost to bursting. Now, to burst is to die. This means that full dedication to the spiritual welfare of neighbours fully overcomes selfish concern.

The dynamism of love is now at its best: the brave followers of Christ hasten along his way. They do not allow either pleasure or pain to stop them because in the union of their will to God's will they enjoy perfect peace. They do not try to hide their virtue under their pretence of humility and are always ready to make use of it on behalf of neighbours. Far from avoiding pain, they enjoy having a share in Christ's passion. Like valiant knights they stay on the battlefield with no shield or weapon but love. Like 'glorious Paul' they find their glory in the persecutions and insults of the crucified: 'suffering is pleasure to them and pleasure is labour'. God 'has his rest' in such souls: he is ever present in them. Being all afire with charity they cannot be injured either by man or devil. Like Christ on his cross, they are at the same time blissful and sorrowful, sorrow being caused by awareness of sin, and bliss by the charity that unites them to God:

> They go after the immaculate Lamb, my only-begotten Son: staying on his cross he was blissful and suffering. Suffering was he in bearing the cross of bodily pain together with the cross of his desire to make satisfaction for the sin of humankind, and blissful because the Godhead united with his humanity could not suffer, and by showing itself without a veil to his human soul filled it with bliss. (D, LXXVIII)

Having thus ascended the way of Christ-the-bridge, his followers have come to share his very inmost sentiments. Still, the imperfection of the mortal condition fosters the desire of a full vision of God's glory in himself and in his creatures such as the soul will enjoy when, through the narrow door, it will merge into the wide peaceful sea, God himself.

Catherine insists on the fact that the Father is not the way 'because no pain can fall on him'; pain falls on Christ, who is the way and model for us. Our way cannot be without thorns: they sprout as the consequence of sin. But the source of the most painful suffering is love itself: an increase in love is increase in suffering.[9] Since the way of the bridge is the way of love, going along it cannot be painless:

> All of you have to go along this bridge by seeking the glory and praise of my name in the salvation of souls, painfully bearing many hardships in the footsteps of this sweet loving Word: by no other way could you come to me. (D, XXIII)

Christ is life. Together with the Father and the Holy Spirit he is 'He who is', essential, eternal life, giving life to whatever exists. He is, as he described it, the vine from which its branches draw life-fostering sap (John 15:1):

> I – says the Father – am the labourer who planted the genuine vine, my only-begotten Son, into the soil of your humanity, so that you, the branches, might bear fruit. (D, XXIII)

He is also the restorer of life in humankind, the life of grace it had lost because of sin. Here Catherine makes use of one of her favourite images, that of the tree of life and the tree of death. God created the human soul as a tree of life, and disobedience turned it into a tree of death, yielding deadly fruit. But God did not permit his most beloved creature to stay in death:

> You, high eternal Trinity . . . seeing that this tree could bear no fruit except deadly ones, since it was parted from you who are life, provided to give it the remedy, as lovingly as you had created it, by grafting your Godhead onto the dead tree, our humanity. O sweetest and most pleasant graft! You, supreme sweetness, have deigned to unite with our bitterness; you, splendour, with darkness; you, wisdom, with foolishness; you, infinite, to us who are finite. Who compelled you to restore life in this creature that

had so badly injured you? Nothing but love . . . so that by this graft death is dissolved. (P, X)

This graft, the assumption of human nature by the Word of God, is just the beginning of his action for the revival of human-kind; it was to be followed by a second one when Christ, bearing the heavy load of sinful humanity, grafted himself to the wood of the cross:

> But was your love appeased by such union? No. Therefore you, eternal Word, watered this tree with your blood. The warmth of this blood makes it sprout, provided that man by his free choice engrafts himself in you, and unites to you his heart and affection, binding the graft tight with the wrapping of charity. (Ibid.)

Without the third engrafting, our own, we could have no share in the life provided by the first and second. We are offered a precious gift, but it is our free choice to accept or refuse it, just as we are expected to choose whether to go on the bridge or to stay.

In a letter to Tommaso d'Alviano, the captain of a company of mercenaries, Catherine presents the redemption of humankind as a new creation that the Father entrusts to his Son to achieve. The letter to this 'most beloved brother in Christ the sweet Jesus' opens with a wish that his service to God may earn eternal lordship for him. Such service is to be enlightened by faith, which opens our mind's eye to the mystery of love in the creation of man, and in his redemption by the sacrifice of God's own Son:

> By his blood we have come to know that he newly created us to grace, which man had lost by his own fault. Out of love, then, God created us in his own image and likeness, and out of love did he give us his Son to bring us back to his grace by creating us anew in his blood. (L, 259)

The image of the Trinity impressed in the human soul had been so disfigured by sin that it could only be restored by the same power which had first moulded it, the power of love. But man had to be made aware of it so that love might be kindled in the soul and restore harmony in the powers which sin had upset. Man had to be created anew by setting before his mind's eye a new proof of God's ineffable love.

> By means of his Son, God wanted to show us his truth, his kind will ever seeking our sanctification. His truth was that he had

created man so that he should partake in his own eternal vision where the soul is made blissful.

Sin hinders the fulfilment of such truth, but God will not give up:

> he compels himself by his charity to give us what he most cherishes, his only-begotten Son, and imposes on him this obedience: to restore man and make him return from death to life. God wants that son, humankind, to be born again, as I said, in blood, and nobody can enjoy the fruit of the blood without the light of faith. This is why Christ said to Nicodemus: 'No man can gain eternal life unless he is born again' (John 3:3). Christ wanted to make known that the eternal Father had granted him to conceive that son, humankind, being impelled by love, and give it birth through true obedience, and hatred and displeasure for the offence to the Father, on the wood of the most holy cross.

We cannot help being reminded of the parable of the prodigal son, except that the roles are reversed. In that story the son is the protagonist: he claims his share in the family estate, goes to a distant country, spends all his money, starves, repents or realizes what a big mistake he has made, decides that he had better go back to his father and be with him, even as a slave, rather than feed pigs. The father, so far, has appeared as rather passive, he has made no effort to dissuade the boy from leaving; but when, seeing him coming from afar, he runs to meet him and welcomes him not as a slave, but as his own beloved child, we can realize how much the son's absence had weighed on him. With Catherine it is the father who causes the rescue of the lost child, and the elder brother, far from resenting his father's loving reception of the prodigal boy, readily accepts the task that is 'given' to him – given as a privilege by a fond father to a faithful son – that of becoming a second father to his brother, and of sharing the father's paternity. The only passive person in the process of rebirth is the sinful son, but, once he is reborn, all the powers in his soul will be restored to harmonious action.

In the story of humankind's rebirth Catherine's attention is naturally focused on the Word of God:

> Indeed this sweet Word seemed to behave like the eagle that stares at the sphere of the sun, and from above sees the food it wants to take: having seen it down on the ground, it comes and snatches it, then eats it on high. Likewise sweet Jesus, our own

eagle, looks into the sun of the Father's eternal will, and sees in it the creature's offence and rebellion, so that in the earth of the creature, which he has come to know from the height of the Father, he has seen the food he is to take. His food is this: for the miserable earth which has offended God with wretched disobedience, he undertakes to fulfil the Father's truth in man, by drawing him from the death-giving slavery of the devil, and bringing him back to serve his Creator. Once, then, he has seen and clutched the food the Father has given him to eat, he sees that it cannot be eaten down on the ground, if miserable man is to be brought back to his former obedience; therefore he rises with his prey to the height of the most holy cross there to eat it with painful, ineffable desire, thus punishing our iniquities in himself, by undergoing pain in his body and making satisfaction by his will, through displeasure and hatred of sin.

To compare the height of the cross to the high rocks where eagles carry their prey and share it with their little ones in the nest, may seem odd. But the cross on Calvary is the summit of love's voluntary suffering, the suffering of God-and-Man. And he, his love being made visible, can draw to himself man's heart and, with it, all the faculties of his soul, thus achieving his rebirth. Then memory is drawn by the Father's might to keep the remembrance of his many gifts; understanding rises to the wisdom of the immaculate Lamb, and comes to know that love is at the root of whatever God permits to happen so that neither adversity nor prosperity can trouble him; affection rushes towards God's love which the mind's eye has shown to it, and love naturally extends from God to neighbour. Being freed from love of self by the Holy Spirit, one is made a faithful servant of his Creator, so that what he loves, he loves for God's sake, whatever his status in life may be.

Coming to the conclusion of the letter, Catherine goes back to the wish she had expressed at its beginning: for service to God in the light of faith as the means to earn lordship not only for future life, but even during our stay on earth:

Faith should be active: 'Faith without good deeds is dead' (James 2:26–27). In no other way could we be servants of Christ crucified, which service makes man reign, both in lasting life and [in the present] by making himself his own lord. In fact, if he masters himself, he is given lordship of the whole world, because he does not care about anything except God, whom he loves and honours. Many are lords of cities and castles, but having no lordship over themselves through love of virtue, they find they have got nothing, being empty both of the world and of God, either in life or death. (L, 259)

The rebirth that Christ has earned for all men is not enjoyed by those who refuse to graft themselves onto the tree of life. When thinking of the actual condition of the world, Catherine feels it is so deep in sin that it is almost dead:

I see the whole world lying down in death, such a bad one that my soul faints at this sight. How, then, can this dead one be called back to life, since you, God impassible, will come no more to rescue the world, but to pass judgement on it? How, then, can life be given back to this dead one? I do not believe, O infinite bounty, that you may be short of remedies; rather, I acknowledge that your love is not lacking, nor has your might grown feeble and your wisdom diminished; therefore you will, can and know how to provide the remedy needed. This is why I beseech you, if it pleases your goodness, to show me the remedy so that my soul may be spurred courageously to make use of it.

Having listened to the response, Catherine resumes her prayer:

Yes, your Son is not to come again, except in majesty, to judge, as has been said. But, as I see, you call your servants 'christs', and by such means you intend to take death away and restore life in the world. By which means? That they go along the way of the Word with manly courage, solicitude and ardent desire towards your honour and the salvation of human souls; patiently bearing, towards this aim, pain, torments, insults, reproaches from anybody. Through such finite sufferings you intend to give comfort to their infinite desire, by granting what they ask and fulfilling their desires. You, excellent giver of remedies, give us such christs, living in constant vigil, tears, prayers for the salvation of the world. You call them your christs because they are conformed to your only-begotten Son. (P, XII)

This explanation was due. In fact, while the word 'christ' is normally used by Catherine for priests who in their sacramental ministry 'act in the person of Christ', she very seldom applies that name to lay people. In the *Dialogue* we read about God's true servants:

They can properly be called another Christ crucified, my only-begotten Son, because they have taken on them his own task. He came as a mediator to put an end to war and reconcile man with me in peace by much suffering up to the shameful death of the cross. Likewise such individuals go about in the sign of the cross making mediators of themselves by prayer and speech, and by offering the example of a good, saintly life. (D, CXLVI)

Every believer who is so united to him through love as to become 'another Christ' can be a giver of life to a sick, almost dead, world. Christ wants every man to share in his work. Since he sets himself as an example for us to imitate and wants us to do so, he has made it possible for us to follow in his footsteps. This is why he enabled his disciples – a handful of men – to go and tell the good news, his own truth, all over the world. He is our leader, the brave captain fighting ahead of his soldiers, of all of us who are on the battlefield of earthly life.

When contemplating Christ many images hustle through Catherine's mind. He is the gallant knight jousting to win the heart of his beloved lady, with rather unusual equipment: his horse is the wood of the cross, his cuirass his own scourged body; for a helmet he has the painful crown of thorns, for a sword the wound in his side, and the lance in his hand is the scornful reed. The red wounds in his hands and feet stand for gloves and spurs. But who furnished him with such unusual weapons? Love, answers Catherine, nothing but love could have made him undergo his passion, and we, who are to fight under his leadership, must have a similar equipment:

> Who can be so faint-hearted that, looking at this captain and knight being slain and victorious at the same time, will not free his heart of cowardice and face any enemy with manly courage? No one. This is why I told you to gaze intensely on Christ crucified. (L, 256)

Christ is the strong wrestler who, in the duel between life and death on the cross, conquered death by being overcome by it: the death of his human body destroyed death of the spirit in human-kind (ibid.).

He is the lamb prefigured in the Old Testament in the deliverance of the Hebrews from slavery, the lamb that had to be roasted on live fire; likewise the immaculate lamb of our rescue is 'roasted by the fire of divine charity on the spit of the most holy cross'.[10]

When speaking of Christ-the-lamb Catherine is never short of adjectives: he is sweet, mild, consummate and immaculate, loving, poor, humble, forlorn, persecuted, tormented, despised, precious. By a singular process of thought from lamb to parchment, Catherine says that Christ tore to pieces in his own body the bond of our servitude to the devil:

> O inestimable, sweetest charity! you have torn up the bond between man and the devil; you have torn it to pieces on the wood of the holy cross. A bond is made of nothing but lamb and this is the immaculate Lamb who inscribed us on himself. But he tore up this bond. (L, 69)[11]

Surprisingly, Catherine shifts from the image of the humble, mild lamb who does not complain when he is being led to slaughter to that of a roaring lion:

> I said I wanted you to be a lamb in following the true Lamb; now I tell you I want you to be a lion loudly roaring in the body of holy Church, so strong in voice and virtue, that you may be of help in calling back to life the children lying dead within it. And, were you to ask: 'Where shall I get such a strong, roaring voice?' From the Lamb, who is silent and quiet in his humanity, but in his Godhead lends power to the cry of the Son with the voice of his boundless charity. So that, by the strength and power of Godhead and of the love that united God to man, by this virtue has the lamb turned lion and, remaining on the chair of the cross, he has shouted so loud to humankind, the dead child, that he has taken death away and given him life. (L, 177)[12]

Many different images are scattered at any one time from Catherine's mind, just like different colours from a diamond when struck by a ray of sunlight. She presents several facets of Christ's kindness to some captives one Holy Thursday: he is the sick patient and the physician, the knight bravely fighting for our rescue and the wet-nurse taking the bitter remedy that the child would not swallow, but will receive without its strong taste through suckling (L, 260).

Another remarkable grouping of different images in as few words as possible is to be found in a letter to Raymond of Capua:

> I want you to enclose yourself in the open side of the Son of God, which is an open storehouse full of perfumes, so that sin itself is made fragrant in it. There the sweet bride rests on the bed of fire and blood; there the secret of the heart of God's

Son is openly to be seen. O you, pierced cask, giving drink and intoxicating all loving desires, giving delight and enlightenment to the understanding, so filling the memory that strives towards you that it cannot either keep, understand or love anything except sweet kind Jesus: blood and fire, inestimable love! (L, 273)

Of the many figures of speech which enliven the expression of Catherine's thought a few are exclusively used for Christ and for his mother as if to stress the intimate link between them. So, Christ all afire with burning desire for the redemption of mankind is seen as a chariot of fire coming down to earth; Mary, too, is a chariot of fire as she carries divine fire within her womb. Christ is the book everybody can read, so plain its characters; and Mary is a book in which the Word of God's doctrine can be read as well: she is the table inscribed by God's finger with the new law, the law of love perfecting the old one.[13] We might be surprised to find that the image of the peaceful sea, an image suggestive of God's immensity, is applied to her:

O Mary, you peaceful sea! Mary, giver of peace!

but less so after reading:

O Mary, Mary, shrine of the Trinity! (P, XI)

The 'peaceful sea' has in her a most cherished dwelling. To raise man's mind to the knowledge of divine mysteries, the Word of God humbled himself to our own earthly level; Mary's humility raised her above herself by making her the object of the eternal Father's special love, and caused her to be chosen for the fulfilment of his plan for the redemption of humankind.[14]

Mary shares her son's mission as revealer of truth: the dignity of human nature in its possession of free choice is given great evidence in God's gentle approach for her consent to the incarnation:

In you, O Mary, are man's fortitude and freedom tested because, after the divine council has so decided, an angel is sent to you to announce the mystery of the divine counsel and seek your consent, nor did the Son of God descend to your womb before your will consented. He was waiting at your will's door, waiting for you to open, because he wanted to come into you, and he would never have entered unless you had opened by saying 'Here is the handmaid of the Lord, be it done to me according to your words' . . . At your door, O Mary, eternal Godhead was knocking but, unless you opened the door of your will, God would not have incarnated himself in you. (P, XI)

Once her consent is given, Mary's will is so united to the will of the Father as to make it impossible for her to do or wish to do anything apart from it, and identity of will makes the link between mother and Son much stronger than a mere physical one.

Catherine considers a double issue in the Holy Spirit's action for the incarnation of the Word: as he is given his human form, the mother's soul is imprinted as if by a seal with the very form of the Spirit of Love:

> I see, O fire of charity, that there is another union: he gets the form of his body and she, like warm wax, has been imprinted with desire and love for our salvation by the seal of the Holy Spirit, the same seal and graft effecting the incarnation of eternal divine Word. She, like a tree of mercy, receives within herself the consummate soul of her son, which soul is wounded by the Father's will, and she, as an engrafted tree, is wounded by the knife of hatred and love. Now, hatred and love have grown so big in the mother and in the son, that he rushes to death because of his great desire to give us life: such is his hunger and so great his desire of saintly obedience to the Father, that he has lost all love of self and rushes to the cross. Likewise that sweetest and dearest mother is willing to lose the loving presence of her son so that, far from dissuading him from dying, as any mother would, she had rather make a ladder of herself, and wants him to die. But no wonder, since she had been wounded by the arrow of love for our salvation. (L, 30)[15]

We might be shocked by Catherine's comment: can Mary's self-denial and severe mastering of motherly affection be considered just a common occurrence? By no means: Catherine points out that her behaviour is not what one might expect from any normal mother. But since Mary's will had been so imprinted by the Holy Spirit with the Father's will, she simply could not have done otherwise: Catherine's way of reasoning is strictly logical. Besides, Catherine's image of Mary in the passion is in tune with that given by the Gospel of her 'standing' by the cross (John 19:25).

By her conscious acceptance of her son's passion Mary was strictly associated with him in the redemption of the world, since his suffering body was her own:

Christ redeemed it with his passion, and you by the pain of your body and mind. (P, XI)

After his death and resurrection, Mary is still contributing to Christ's mission with generous self-denial. Both she and the apostles might have enjoyed staying together, but since they had to go and spread the good news all over the world, she readily accepted being left all alone. This was a good example to set before the eyes of Lapa, Catherine's own mother, who could scarcely understand why her daughter should do all that travelling, and was angry about her delayed return from Avignon:

> I want you to learn from Mary, the sweet mother: for the honour of God and our salvation, she gave us her son [to be] slain on the wood of the most holy cross. Having been left alone when Christ ascended to heaven, she stayed with his holy disciples. No doubt that Mary and they enjoyed staying together, and that parting was unpleasant; still, for the glory and praise of her son and the welfare of the whole world, she consents, and wants them to go; she prefers the anxiety of their parting to the comfort she might have had from their staying. (L, 240)

Mary's name is normally associated with that of Christ crucified in the opening of Catherine's letters, and the *Dialogue* has its beginning on 'Mary's day', a Saturday. She shares extreme poverty with Jesus, to the point that when he is born she is short of warm clothing for her baby:

> You see this sweet loving Word being born in a stable, as Mary was on her way, to show you, the travellers, that you must ever be born again in the stable of the knowledge of self, where you will find me, born through grace in your souls. You see him remaining there in the midst of animals, in such poverty that Mary lacked clothing for him and, since the weather was chilly, she warmed him with the breath of animals, and by wrapping him in hay. (D, CLI)

A rather short passage in the *Dialogue* is of help in understanding Catherine's position with regard to the mother of Christ. Its relevance can be better understood if we note that it stands as a hinge between the two sections of the teaching about divine Providence: the first is a sort of historical review of the events in the Old Testament that were aimed at keeping the hope of redemption alive in the people; the second has its beginning in the incarnation and shows God's incessant care to help every single soul to its perfection. At this very important stage Catherine is given an answer to her fourth petition, that about a particular event. After a complaint about human blindness pretending to pass judgement on what it cannot understand, the Lord comes to the 'particular event', that of the young man sentenced to death whom Catherine visited in jail and assisted even to the scaffold.[16]

> I want you to know that to save him from eternal damnation to which, as you know, he was already doomed, I permitted that event so that, by means of his own blood, he should have life in the blood of my Truth. In fact, I had not forgotten his reverence and love for Mary, the most sweet mother of my only-begotten Son. Out of regard for the Word, she has been granted by my bounty that whoever, either just or sinner, holds her in due reverence, shall never be stolen away and devoured by the infernal devil. She is a sort of bait, which my kindness has set before reasonable creatures to catch them. (D, CXXXIX)

A bait: yet another image that Mary shares with her Son, but with a difference, since the bait of Christ's humanity causes the devil to be caught by the hook inside, invisible Godhead, while Mary's bait has no hook at all, its task being not to destroy the enemy, but to draw beloved children to the very source of life. And this has to be done in a gentle, motherly way. But the gentle mother will prove a skilful defender of her children whenever the 'infernal devil' may try to bite. Thus does Catherine synthesize the rich medieval literature about the unceasing struggle between Mary and the enemy of mankind, a struggle unfailingly ending in her victory, all in favour of whoever has paid her even slight homage. But why is she granted such power? 'Out of regard for the Word', her son: the divine maternity accounts for all her privileges. The contents of this short passage are almost as good as a treatise on Mariology.

When approaching the end of his long pilgrimage, Dante is asked by St Bernard, his guide for its last stage, to look at the face which is most like Christ's, because nothing but its clarity can prepare him for the vision of Christ's own face.[17] Catherine too is aware of the fact that Mary is the best insight for us into the mystery of the Word incarnate, in which she is so intimately involved, her physical features being simply a mirror of the inmost communion of spirit. And Mary knows that the almost boundless power granted 'out of regard for the Word' is given her on behalf of mankind, for whose sake the Son of God became her own child.

More than any other creature reaching the third step of the bridge, Mary is impelled towards the welfare of her neighbours by the dynamism of love, and has a most active share in the mission of her Son, who is the 'way and truth and life'. She sheds the light of truth, the truth of divine love, by the union of her will to the will of the Father, in the gift of his and her own Son, for the redemption of humankind; she leads the way to Christ-the-way by her example in following close on his footsteps; with him, and by her share in his passion, she offers a unique contribution to the rescue of human souls from death to life and lovingly helps them to fullness of life.

In concluding the *Dialogue* the mysterious voice speaking to Catherine bears witness to the centrality of Christ, 'Way, Truth and Life', in the story of mankind and in that of every human being:

> Now I, eternal Father, supreme and eternal Truth, tell you in conclusion that in the obedience of the Word, my only-begotten Son, you have life. And as from the first man, the old one, all of you were infected with death, so all who take the key of obedience have gained life from the new man, Christ the sweet Jesus of whom I made a bridge for you because the way to heaven was interrupted. By going along this sweet straight way with the key of obedience, you get through the darkness of the world without any harm. And finally, with the Word's key, you unlock heaven.

Then a final admonishment to Catherine to appreciate properly and use what she has been taught: a doctrine summed up in Christ:

> Be careful never to leave the cell of knowledge of yourself, but in the same cell keep and spend the treasure I have given you, which is the doctrine on truth, founded on the living stone, Christ the sweet Jesus, clad in light discerning through darkness. (D, CLXVI)

And Catherine's response will be a hymn of gratitude and praise to the blessed Trinity and an intense prayer that she may be clad in eternal Truth and hasten in the way of obedience, Christ's own way, in the light of most holy faith, her soul being intoxicated by that light.

Notes

1. Cf. John 14:6.
2. Cf. L. 16.
3. Cf. *Paradiso*, IV, 124ff.
4. The wound made in Christ's side by the lance of a Roman soldier (John 19:34) is often referred to by Catherine as an opening into 'the cave of his chest' for us to be made aware of 'the secret of the heart': the love that led Christ to undergo passion and death. But here she does not seem to hint at that wound: it is the inward fire of love that bursts his side open.
5. In fourteenth-century manuscripts red and blue normally alternate in capital characters, while red is more commonly used to mark the beginning of paragraphs.
6. Here Catherine indulges in a pun upon *seguitare* (to follow) and *perseguitare* (to persecute), which has no equivalent in English.
7. The Jerusalem Bible has 'all men', but the text Catherine could refer to is that of the Vulgate, which reads *omnia*. She may even have heard Thomas Aquinas's comment, *Sup. Io*. 1674: 'He says: "everything" not "everybody" because all are not drawn. "I shall draw everything", I should say, can stand for "soul and body" or "all kinds of men".'
8. Cf. L, 146.
9. Cf. D, V.
10. Cf. L, 52.
11. For a proper understanding of this passage we must remember that *carta* can mean a 'bond' or 'charter' as well as a 'sheet of paper', the material on which the bond is written. Then, since parchment was more likely to be used for important documents, and parchment is made of sheepskin, the chain of thought leads Catherine to the lamb without much effort: Christ tore the bond to pieces by allowing himself to be torn on the cross.
12. According to some medieval bestiaries, lion cubs are not alive when born; only after three days does the lion's powerful roar wake them to life.
13. Cf. L, 259: 'God's holy law, which was given to Moses, founded on fear ... Then came the sweet loving Word with the law of love, not to dissolve the old one, but to perfect it, since fear did not give us life. But he so reconciled them as to make perfect the imperfect one.'
14. Cf. P, IV; P, XI.
15. The same concept as found in L, 144: 'Mary ... could wish for nothing but the honour of God and the salvation of the creature ... and this is why, short of other means, she would have liked to make a ladder of herself to help her son to the cross.'
16. In L, 273 Catherine relates to Raymond her action on behalf of the anonymous youth, who is currently identified as the Perugian Niccolò di Tuldo. Striking coincidence in wording makes it very probable that the event here hinted at is the same.
17. Cf. *Paradiso*, XXXII, 85ff.

6

Catherine and the Church

> The church is Christ
> himself. (L, 171)

When Catherine was about six years old, as she was coming home after spending the afternoon with one of her married sisters, she was taken by surprise by a wonderful vision: high above the church of St Dominic, on the opposite side of Valle Piatta, she saw the Lord Jesus Christ, in beautiful pontifical vestments, and with him the apostles Peter, Paul and John. The Lord smiled amiably at her as his right hand blessed her with the sign of the cross (*Life*, 29–30).

It was the beginning of a lifelong love story: Catherine fell in love with the great pontiff who had so kindly smiled at the little girl that she was, and who had given her his special blessing. From that moment she could love nobody but Christ, but having realized that pontiff and Church are one, love for Christ must at the same time be love for his Church. She had seen that Christ is the pontiff and the pontiff is Christ. This is why she afterwards coined her own phrase for the Pope: 'Christ-on-earth'.

Some twenty-five years later her childish intuition was to be confirmed and explained by the mysterious voice that spoke to her in the *Dialogue*. After the description of Christ-the-bridge, an objection is proposed: yes, I understand – you might say – Christ made a bridge of himself by the assumption of human nature in his divine person, and made of himself a safe way for us, but by his ascension to heaven he left our world: what about the way, now?

After he rose and came back to me, the Father, I sent the Teacher, the Holy Spirit, who had with him my power, the wisdom of my Son, and his own, the Holy Spirit's, clemency. He is one with me, the Father, and with my Son. He strengthened the way of the doctrine which my Truth had bequeathed to the world and therefore, when his presence departed, neither his doctrine nor his virtues, the genuine stones founded on this doctrine, were removed; this is the way this sweet and glorious bridge has built for you. . . .

That doctrine was confirmed by the clemency of the Holy Spirit who gave such fortitude to the minds of the disciples as enabled them to bear witness to the truth and proclaim the way, the doctrine of Christ crucified. (D, XXIX)

The meaning of these words is evident: on leaving the world Christ passes his own role as 'bridge' to his Church whose life has its beginning with the descent of the Holy Spirit on the apostles. And they, without delay, begin to preach the happy news, the doctrine of Christ crucified. Such doctrine

has been confirmed by the apostles and declared in the blood of martyrs, clarified by the doctors and attested by confessors and written by the evangelists. All these stand as witnesses to attest the truth in the mystical body of holy Church. They are lamps placed on the lamp-stand to show the way of truth leading to life with perfect light. And how do they tell you this? Through testing, because they tested it in themselves. . . . You see, then, that this true doctrine has remained as a boat to help human souls past the stormy sea and lead them to a safe haven.

The image of the boat, a traditional symbol of the Church, should solve any doubt about the identity of the bridge which was offered to humankind after Christ ascended to heaven. The efficiency of his new bridge is due to its disposing of the might of the Father, the wisdom of the Son and the loving clemency of the Holy Spirit:

Such might lends the virtue of fortitude to those who go along this way; wisdom gives them light to understand the truth in the same way, and the Holy Spirit gives them such love as wears away and removes any sensual love from the soul, and love of virtue alone is left. So that in every way, in his own person or by his doctrine, he is way and truth and life.

This is how Christ fulfilled his promise to come back to his disciples after ascending to the Father:

He said he would come back and he did, because the Holy Spirit was not alone: he had with himself the might of the Father, the wisdom of the Son and his own clemency.

Thus did the three divine Persons strengthen the way of the doctrine:

> which way cannot fail or be hindered from those who want to follow it, because it is firmly set and proceeds from me, who am immovable. Therefore you must not hesitate in going along this way, or suffer any cloud to dim the light of faith which was given you in the shape of a vestment in holy baptism.
>
> Now have I shown and explained to you all about the personal bridge and the doctrine, which is one with the bridge, and have told those who might ignore it who shows them that this is the way of truth, and where are those who teach it. And I said that such were the apostles and evangelists, the martyrs and confessors and saintly doctors, standing as lamps in holy Church. (D, XXIX)[1]

A similar list of witnesses to the truth of Christ's doctrine includes another category, that of the virgins who in their charity, purity and obedience:

> proclaim the obedience of the Word, showing the perfection of obedience as it shines in my Truth who, because of the obedience I imposed on him, hurried to the shameful death on the cross. (D, LXXXV)

The statement that Christ's doctrine is the bridge offered to mankind as long as there will be human beings on earth poses the identity of Christ and his Church and sets forth the strength of the Church, since it can rely on the power of the Father, the wisdom of the Son and the Holy Spirit's enlightening love. In addition, the list of the different members of the Church expected to be 'lamps' shedding the light of Christ's doctrine means that all those who go along the bridge can, or must, help in proclaiming the Gospel. This engagement comes from the general priesthood, which is conferred by baptism. But, alongside the ministry of doctrine, the Church is also entrusted with the ministry of the sacraments which is reserved to priests.

In two chapters of the *Dialogue* which precede the description of the bridge, the distinction of the two ministries is clearly stated under the image of the vineyard: every human being is given a vine, his own soul, and has to take care of it, not only on his own account, but also for the sake of his neighbours, each vine being so close to the others that any disease it might contract would easily spread to them:

> You are my labourers – says the Lord – having been set by me to work in the vineyard of holy Church. You work in the universal body of Christian religion, where I graciously placed you, having granted you the light of holy baptism which you received in the mystical body of holy Church from the hands of my ministers, whom I set to work together with you. You are in the universal body and they are in the mystical body, [their task being] to pasture your souls by ministering the blood [of Christ] in the sacraments that you receive from her [the Church], by uprooting the thorns of mortal sin and planting grace in them. They are the labourers in the vineyard of your souls, bound to the vineyard of holy Church. (D, XXIII)[2]

The ministry of the sacraments is represented by a small building standing on the bridge; in it the body and the blood of Christ are kept and distributed to passers-by so that they may not faint on the way. Another important hint at the ministry is given in the praise of divine mercy closing this section of the *Dialogue*. After recalling God's gifts to humankind from creation to redemption, and after recalling God's never-ceasing providential care of every single person, Catherine exclaims:

> I see that your mercy compelled you to give man even more by leaving yourself as food, so that the feeble creatures that we are should be comforted, and the unmindful ignorant might not lose the remembrance of your bounty. And this is why you give it every day, making yourself present in the sacrament of the altar, in the mystical body of holy Church. Who did this? Your mercy. (D, XXX)

The mention of the Eucharist as a reminder of Christ's passion is of peculiar importance at this point, when attention is turned from the description of the bridge itself to that of its ascent by various stages corresponding to progress in love, a progress to be fostered by the remembrance of God's love, whose most evident expression is the sacrifice of his own Son on the cross.

The presentation of the bridge is followed and completed by the teaching about the Church as being the trustee of Christ's doctrine. Similarly the teaching about the ascent of the bridge leads to an instruction about the Church in its ministry of the sacraments. After giving thanks to God for what she has come to know about the growth of the soul from imperfect to most perfect love, Catherine asks to be told about the misdoings of the clergy so that she may be spurred to more intense prayer and penance on their behalf.

The answer begins with praise of the Eucharist, God's supreme gift to man enhancing the nobility of noble human nature, and lending special dignity to ministers. Here, at the end of the ascent where growth in love is conditioned by enlightenment of the mind, the sacrament of the body and blood of Christ is compared to the sun, the greatest source of light a normal person in Catherine's time might think of. The sun is also a symbol of incorruption: it can throw its rays all day long on mud and garbage and remain unsoiled. Likewise the virtue of the sacrament will not be diminished by its being administered by an unworthy priest. Another example from light follows, that of a lamp losing nothing of its light when it kindles other lamps: the light thus shared will be proportional to the capacity of the lamps. If a number of persons went to light candles of various sizes from a burning one, its flame would not be dimmed thereby, and each candle would have a flame of similar colour and shape, but bigger flames would be burning at the end of bigger candles. This means that though the sacrament is perfect in itself, the results of our approach to it will be proportional to our disposition, or to the intensity of our desire. The material we are made of is naturally disposed to feed the flame, like the wax in a candle:

Your material is love – says the Lord – because I created you out of love, and this is why you cannot live without love.

But the wax would not burn unless the candle had a wick inside. Now, what kind of wick should we have so that our own 'wax' may burn?

This being, given you out of love, has been conditioned [to burn] in holy baptism . . . Without that you could not share this light; you would be like a candle without the wick inside: it cannot receive the light and burn. So would you be if you did not have in your soul most holy faith, the wick that receives the light.

Divine charity is the perennial source of fire and light for human souls to quench their thirst by loving and fearing God, and following the doctrine of Christ:

In fact, it will burn more or less bright according to the material it brings and offers to the fire, since, though all of you are made of the same material ... each one may grow in love and virtue after my pleasure and yours. (D, CX)

When the Eucharist is received with the due disposition of desire and purity, such intimate and vital union is achieved between God and the soul as that of 'a fish in the sea and the sea in a fish', and the divine presence leaves such an imprint on it as does a seal on soft-ened wax; the divine likeness is then restored in the soul, which is the goal of the ascent along the bridge. This is why this first section of the speech on the 'mystical body' appears to be complementary to the 'Doctrine on the Bridge', explaining how the human soul can rise to perfection by degrees, through enlightenment of the mind that fosters increase in love. The images from light here employed – the sun, the candles – recall Catherine's summing up in her thanksgiving all she has learnt as a gift of light:

To me, imperfect and plunged in darkness, you, perfection and light, have shown perfection and the luminous way: the doctrine of your only-begotten Son. (D, CVIII)

But what about a person receiving the sacrament in mortal sin?

That soul is like a candle on which water has fallen: it just hisses when brought near to fire: no sooner has fire got into it than it is extinguished, and nothing but smoke is left in the candle.

The situation of that soul is, then, worse than it was before receiving the Eucharist, but the sacrament is not diminished in itself or soiled.

You see, then, that by no means can such light and its colour and warmth be parted, neither for lack of desire in him who receives it nor because of faults in the minister: I have already told you that the sun is not soiled by its rays hitting impure objects. (D, CX)

The invulnerability of the Eucharist and of the other sacraments is here duly stressed: the faults of the clergy, which are now to be dealt with, might lead one to doubt whether such wicked persons can validly undertake the ministry. Yes, they can, says Catherine, because the power they have been given when ordained does not depend on personal qualities. But to use it with an evil conscience is certainly very culpable. She then insists upon the dignity of priesthood: if priests properly understood it, they would never spoil it by sinful behaviour. They have been chosen and anointed to be 'other Christs', acting in the name of Christ himself, and he wants them to be pure, humble, open-hearted. They should never, for instance, exact money for their ministry. The flock has to provide for the needs of the pastor, since what he gives is far more valuable than the material help he may receive. Offerings are to be used for the maintenance of the church and the needs of the pastor, but the poor should have a large share in them. Good pastors were, and are, aware of their great responsibility in having been entrusted with the ministry of the sacraments, as they draw their virtue from the blood that Christ shed in his passion:

> To whom did he [Christ] leave the keys to his blood? To Peter, the glorious apostle, and to the others who came or will come: until doomsday they have, and will have, the same authority that was Peter's. No fault of theirs can diminish it, or steal away perfection from that blood and the sacraments. (D, CXV)

Together with the keys of the 'cellar' where the blood is kept – a symbol of the Church as depository of the eucharistic wine – Peter was given the authority to call others to help him in the ministry: it is his duty to recall and correct them whenever necessary. Their misdemeanours should not become an excuse for civil authorities to persecute the Church, as often happens:

> Because of the high dignity and authority I have bestowed on them they are exempted from servitude or subjection to the lordship of temporal lords. Civil law has nothing to do with them as regards punishment; punishment only belongs to him who has been placed to govern and administer after divine law.[3] Such are my anointed, and therefore did I say in Holy Scriptures: 'Do not touch my anointed ones' (Ps 105:15). (D, CXV)

This sin, we are told, is one of the worst, since it is not bred by ignorance or passion but by sheer malice, and is aimed at Christ himself. However, like the poisoned arrow wounding the archer, the offence turns back on the offenders.

By way of relief, Catherine is then told about good ministers: having clad themselves with the true Sun and filled the powers of their souls with it, they mirror its ways:

The sun enlightens and warms the earth and makes it sprout; likewise these sweet ministers of mine, elected, and anointed, and set in the mystic body of holy Church to administer me, the Sun, which is to say the body and blood of my only-begotten Son and the other sacraments, all getting their vitality from this blood ... they shed light in the mystic body of holy Church: the light of supernatural science enlivened by the colour of a righteous and honest life, in the footsteps of my Truth's teaching, and they minister the warmth of most ardent charity. Their warmth and the light of their science caused sterile souls to flourish. By their saintly and orderly life, they expelled the darkness of mortal sins and of infidelity, and put order in the lives of those who had been living without any rule in the darkness of sin, chilled by lack of charity. You see, then, that they are suns, whose qualities they borrow from me, the true Sun, and are made one with me and I with them under the action of love. (D, CXIX)

The champions presented to Catherine as living examples of conformity to the divine Sun are, first, three Popes: Peter, who preached Christ's doctrine and bore it witness with his blood; Gregory the Great, for his knowledge of Holy Scripture and his saintly life; Sylvester, who was granted special grace for success in his disputes with the infidels. To this trio of excellent pastors, there follows a trio of excellent doctors in the persons of Augustine, Thomas Aquinas and Jerome: by uprooting errors in true and perfect humility, they threw flashes of light on the Bride of Christ like lamps placed on the lamp-stand.

To join exemplary pastors and doctors in the common praise of good priests is one way to state that, though lay believers have a share in the ministry of truth, both ministries, doctrinal and sacramental, are proper to the priesthood. Special praise is given to ecclesiastical authorities when they are particularly careful in correcting their subjects, which requires courage and purity of conscience because correction falls short of its aim when the corrector is deep in the same abuses he pretends to redress. Such good pastors were eager for God's honour and the salvation of creatures, they savoured this food on the table of the most holy cross. Prelates rendered glory to God, and displeasure to themselves for their misdemeanours and justice to their subjects. They were true followers of the good Shepherd who gave his life for his flock, and in healing wounds they knew how to mitigate hard remedies with gentleness of touch. Justice, the maintainer of a state under civic or divine law, was shining on them like a pearl; justice has to be done to prevent one corrupt member from corrupting the whole body.

> But they do not do so, today; they even pretend they do not see. Do you know why? Because the root of love of self is still alive, and from it sprouts wicked servile fear. In fact, being afraid of losing temporary advantages, they do not correct; they act as if they had been blinded, and do not understand how a status has to be kept. If they saw that it is to be held by justice, they would strive for it . . . Also, they do not correct because they are aware of being in the same and worse faults. (D, CXIX)

Exemplary ministers are lovers of voluntary poverty, patient in bearing injury, attentive to the needs of subjects, offering for them prayer, and to them teaching and the example of a good life: authentic guardian angels. They are fearless because, remaining in God's love, they share in the wisdom of the Son, the power of the Father, which gives them strength to face tyrants, and the burning love of Holy Spirit.

> You see, then, they were not alone . . . and therefore had no fear. Only the man who feels alone, who has no hope except in himself, being deprived of the love of charity, is afraid: every trifle will frighten him. (Ibid.)

More hideous than leaving abuses unpunished is the hypocrisy which tries to conceal cowardice under an appearance of justice:

> And sometimes they will correct, just to put on that scant justice as a cloak, and instead of aiming at one in high position who, maybe, is more guilty than another at a lower social level, fearing he [the powerful one] may become an obstacle to their position or ways of life, they will turn to one not so important because they see that he could not harm them and remove them from office. Such injustice they do because of their miserable love of self. (D, CXXII)

Such a lover of truth as Catherine was must have despised hypocrisy as the basest and most repugnant of vices.

Now attention is turned to ministers who do not fulfil their duties. Catherine is given a full answer to her request to be made aware of the misdemeanours of the clergy, so that she may pray more fervently for priests. But before the crude description of their faults, she insists upon the dignity of the priesthood and its not being dependent on personal qualities. A minister might be a 'devil incarnate', and still respect should be paid to him. This foundation having been firmly established, the sad reality need not be concealed. Ministers are proud, greedy; they are too fond of precious furniture for their houses and fine big horses for their sport; they indulge in rich food and all sorts of luxury. Of the alms they receive they should make three parts: for the maintenance of their church, for the poor and for their own needs, but they monopolize practically the whole of them. They are so eager for money that they do not mind indulging in usury. They should be as pure as angels, and are anything but that. Instead of being careful for the spiritual welfare of their flock, they will induce to sin, because the dog of their conscience is asleep, having grown faint for lack of food. They can be said to rival the devil in depriving their subjects of the life of grace:

> they cause painful pangs of conscience in those whom they lure from the state of grace and the way of truth and, by leading them to sin, make them go along the way of falsehood. (D, CXXI)

Some are grown so devilish that they have become unmindful of the honour due to the sacrament and of their own dignity, and practise black magic. (D, CXXVI)

Still, in spite of their misbehaviour, such wicked ministers seem to be reliable when they teach orthodox doctrine:

> in accordance with what my Truth said in holy Gospel (Matt 23:3) you must do what they tell you – [which is to say] the doctrine given to you in the mystical body of holy Church as offered in accordance with Holy Scripture by the criers: the preachers who have to proclaim my word – and avoid imitating their evil ways . . . Leave their wicked life to them and accept the doctrine. (D, CXXI)

However, they are so plunged in darkness that they cannot see beyond the 'bark' of Holy Scripture (its literal meaning) and, their spiritual taste having been spoilt by pride and lust, they do not savour its contents. This is why their sermons have little or no impact on the people: they simply produce 'a sound of words' that does not reach to the heart:

> Their preaching is aimed rather at pleasing people and delighting their ears than at giving me honour, because, instead of striving

for an honest life, all their concern is for clever speech. (D, CXXV)

Having spoilt and soiled the mirror of good behaviour, they will earn for themselves most severe punishment, while good ministers will be specially rewarded because they let the light of holy science illuminate their souls and foster their love:

> the more one knows, the more one loves, and he who loves better gets more. Your merit is weighed on the scale of love. (D, CXXXI)

Catherine's thanksgiving at the end of the doctrine of the mystical body is a warm hymn of gratitude for the insight into the mystery of Christ, 'all God and all man' permanently given to mankind in the Eucharist, and a passionate plea for mercy for the world and for the Church:

> Alas, for my miserable, sorrowful soul, the cause of every evil! Do not delay in granting mercy to the world: accept the desires of your servants and respond to them. Alas! it is you who make them entreat: do listen to their voice . . .
>
> The fire of your charity must not, even cannot, refrain from opening to those who insist on knocking at your door. Open, then, unlock the hardened hearts of your creatures; not in response to them, since they do not knock, but do it because of your servants who knock in their stead. Yield to them, eternal Father: you see them staying at the door of your Truth and entreating you.
>
> And what are they seeking? The blood of the door, your Truth. His blood is ours since you bathed us in it. You cannot and do not want to refuse it to those who ask for it in truth . . .
>
> Do give, then, the fruit of the blood to your creatures, put the price of your Son's blood on the scales so that infernal devils may not steal your sheep away. Oh, you are a good shepherd and gave us the true Shepherd, your only-begotten Son, and he, in obedience to you, gave his life for your sheep and bathed us in his blood. This is the blood that in their hunger your servants ask for at your door, and beg you by the same blood, to have mercy on the world, so that holy Church may newly bloom with good and saintly pastors, whose perfume may drive out the stink of the evil rotten ones. (D, CXXXIV)

This prayer is the conclusion of the teaching on the mystical body and of the whole 'Doctrine on the Bridge'. It is a clear insight into

Catherine's feelings about the Church and its being badly in need of reform, not in itself but in its members, and especially in the clergy. It mirrors Catherine's love and faith, and her burning desire that beauty and purity should be restored to the Bride of Christ by such reform. Her desire was to cause action:

> How could I enjoy seeing that life eternal would be given to me and death to your people? and that darkness should rise in your Bride, who is light itself, because of my own faults and of those of your creatures? (D, XIII)

About two years before she dictated her *Dialogue*, in the spring of 1376, Catherine had sent a letter to Pope Gregory XI, then in Avignon, begging him to be a peacemaker in that troubled world, and proposing to him a threefold way of action: first of all, the reform of the Church:

> in the garden of the Church you, its governor, should uproot stinking flowers, full of impurity and greed, swelling with pride: the bad pastors and rectors who poison the garden and make it putrid. Alas! Do you, our governor, make use of your power, uproot these flowers, and throw them away, that they may not govern any longer. See that they attend to governing themselves in saintly and virtuous life. Plant in this garden sweet-scented flowers: pastors and rectors who may prove true servants of Jesus Christ, with no other concern but the honour of God and the salvation of souls, and to be fathers to the poor. (L, 206)

The second proposal, to bring the papal seat back to Rome, is strictly connected to the first because, while it remained in France, political influences weighed too heavily on the choice of prelates for the reform to be achieved. The aim of the third, to proclaim a Crusade, was to deliver the Holy Sepulchre from Saracen dominion, relieve Europe from the bands of mercenary soldiers by sending them to fight in the Holy Land, and put a stop to the Muslim advance in the Balkans.

In the majority of the letters Catherine sent to Pope Gregory she insists on his duty to devote himself to attaining peace by acting on her advice:

> God expects you to provide justice for the many iniquities which are being committed by those who nourish themselves from the garden of holy Church: he says that animals should not feed on man's food. Since he has given you authority, and you

have accepted it, you have to make use of your privileges and power; if you are unwilling to do so, it would be better for you to renounce them, so as better to give honour to God and save your soul. (L, 255)

The spiritual welfare of the flock has to be held far above material advantages:

If you are bound to recover the valuable lordship of the cities you have lost, so much more are you bound to get back the many sheep, which are a treasure for the Church; to lose them is badly to impoverish [the Church] . . . It would be better for us to lose temporal gold, than spiritual wealth . . . Peace, peace then, for the sake of Christ crucified! Do not consider the ignorance, blindness, pride of your children!

War weighs heavily on the people and is an obstacle to the reform of the Church:

The scant resources of the poor are spent in hiring soldiers, who are destroyers of goods and of people. And, as I see, it hinders your project to reform your bride . . . by means of good pastors and rectors. Which, as you know, you could scarcely do in time of war because, being in need of help from princes and lords, you would feel as if you were bound to choose pastors according to their wishes, not your own. An assumed need is, however, the worst of all motives, when it is a matter of appointing pastors or any other Church officers, for choosing persons void of virtue, seekers of personal advantages, instead of those who apply themselves to give glory and honour to God . . . You are in need of help from Christ crucified . . . and he seems to want his Church to go back to its primitive sweet condition . . . by means of true, virtuous pastors and humble servants of God: they can be found, if it pleases your Holiness to look for them. There are two causes for the loss of Church temporal property: war and lack of virtue. In fact, where virtue is lacking, man is always at war with his Creator. (L, 209)

In another letter, when pleading the cause of the Florentine rebels, far from excusing their rebellion, Catherine does not hesitate to point out the responsibility of the French papal legates, whose misgovernment had caused them to rebel (L, 196).

When urging Gregory not to wait any longer to return the papal see to Rome Catherine's words are decisive, authoritative:

You have to come: come, then! Come quietly and do not be afraid. And supposing your closest friends were trying to dissuade you, boldly reply with the words that Christ said to Peter when he was trying affectionately to make him avoid his passion; Christ turned to him and said: 'Away from me, Satan! In your trying to hinder me you would make me seek what belongs to men, not what comes from God. Should I not fulfil my Father's will?' (L, 223)[4]

With high-ranking prelates, as with the Pope, Catherine insists on their duty to contribute to the reform of the Church by keeping their eyes wide open to the misbehaviour of the clergy, so that a stop may be put to it. The damage which is being done to the Church by its members should be shouted out 'with a hundred thousand tongues' (L, 16). An important churchman is frankly told that he must start by freeing himself from the faults he has to correct in others:

You must be a sweet-smelling flower, not a stinking one, and clothe yourself in the whiteness of purity, perfumed with patience and most ardent charity; you are to be open-hearted and generous and learn from first Truth who was so generous as to give his own life . . . I want you to be strong, since God has made of you a pillar in his holy Church. Is there any means of strengthening our feebleness? Surely, by love . . . by setting all our affection and desire on what is stronger than we are: on God, from whom we get fortitude. He, our God, loved us without having been loved, so that as soon as someone has found and savoured such sweet love, he cannot approach or wish any other; apart from him there is nothing he may look for and want. (L, 101)

To another important prelate Catherine writes:

Give yourself, now, a rule of virtuous behaviour, keeping deep in your heart God's love for you, as shown on the cross; preferring death rather than to offend the Creator or to shut your eyes to the offences of your subjects. . . . And when it is time to make new pastors and cardinals, they are not to be chosen out of flattery or money or simony, but entreat him [the Pope] as well as you can, to look for and value whether a man is of good and saintly reputation, wherever he can find one, no matter whether noble or not, because virtue is what makes a man noble and pleasant to God. This is the sweet labour, father, that I beg you, as I have already done, to undertake. And though other labours may be praiseworthy, this is the best of all. (L, 109)

Even a hasty review of Catherine's letters would show her deep concern for the welfare of the Church and how she fostered its renewal. She was not contented with just urging the Pope or high-ranking prelates to act towards that end; she also took care to grow new whole plants for the 'garden'. This is why the contribution of her disciples to Church renewal should not be undervalued.

With Urban VI Catherine's approach was somewhat different. Gregory had been a mild, shy, gentle sort of man, too slow, perhaps, for Catherine's expectations. Urban, on the contrary, had a strong character and straightforward, not to say harsh, manners. He was perhaps too eager to repress abuses, so that she had to ask him to check his violent impulses.

Mitigate, for the sake of Christ crucified, the sudden impulses of your nature. By holy virtue you shall control nature. Since God has given you a naturally big heart, I beg you, and want you, to try your best and make it supernaturally great; I mean that, through zeal and desire for virtue and reformation of holy Church, you may acquire a manly heart grounded on humility.

In his right desire for renewal of the Church, Urban was impatient to see the results of his efforts, and Catherine reminds him:

You cannot at one stroke remove the personal transgressions which are daily made among Christians, and chiefly in the clergy, whom you have to watch more carefully, but you can and must do your best to that end, otherwise you would have the sins of the clergy on your conscience. (L, 364)

In another letter she warns Urban to ascertain the moral quality of those who might present to him candidates for church offices, and listen to good advisers:

Be patient, most holy Father, whenever someone might advise you on this matter, his only aim being God's honour and your own welfare. This is what any child should do; if he loves his father he cannot suffer anything to damage or be of shame to him; but in his solicitude he is ever alert, because he is well aware that a father who has to govern a large family cannot see more than a single man does; this is why, unless his children were careful of their father's honour and welfare, he might often be cheated. You are father and lord of the universal body of the Christian religion, we are, all of us, under the wings of your Holiness; your authority is boundless, but your insight is just that of one man . . . I know that your Holiness earnestly desires to have helpers that may be of help, but you should be patient and listen to them. (L, 302)

In spite of Catherine's wise counsels, Urban's harsh manners made him many enemies: only a few months after he had been elected, the French cardinals, nostalgic for the easy luxurious life at the Avignon court, held a new conclave and elected Cardinal Robert of Geneva as Pope,[5] thus beginning the Great Schism which was to split Western Christianity for about forty years. This new injury to the welfare of the Church was a hard blow for Catherine. Urban called her to Rome where she spent the last months of her life, doing her best to rally Christians to the lawful Pope about whose legitimacy she had no doubt. The reasons for her conviction are clearly stated in the letter addressed to the three Italian cardinals who had given their allegiance to the antipope on the excuse that Urban's election was not valid because it had been made during the stress of a riot by the Romans who wanted to have a 'Roman or at least Italian Pope'. No, says Catherine, the man they presented to the angry people to soothe them was the only Roman among the cardinals, absolutely too old to assume such a heavy responsibility. But Urban was elected the next day, when the riot was over and they had no reason at all to be afraid. Then she frankly puts before their eyes the true cause of their treason: they are unwilling to accept Urban's reproaches:

you know the truth, that Pope Urban is indeed Pope, supreme Pontiff, elected by regular election, not out of fear, in fact more by divine inspiration than through your human contrivances. This is what you proclaimed to us, and this is the truth. Now you have turned away like vile and miserable knights: your very shadow has frightened you.

They cannot be excused as having been deceived by false information since they did not learn the news from others: they gave it to the people:

You might say: 'Why do you not believe me? We know the truth better than you, because we elected him, not you.' And I answer that it is you that are proving your deviation from the truth in many ways, so that I must not believe you when you say that Pope Urban is not the true Pope. If I look back at your life, I do not find it so good and saintly that your conscience should make you avoid lying.

They first said the Urban was Pope, paid homage to him, asked favours of him and made use of them; now they say he is not the lawful Pope: by contradicting themselves they prove that they are liars, and liars are not to be believed. The true reason for their rebellion is to be found in their pride and love of pleasure.

You could not bear, I do not say actual correction, but even a harsh word of reproach made you raise your heads. This is the cause of your change. And that such is the truth appears from the fact that before Christ-on-earth began to bite, you acknowledged and revered him as the vicar of Christ that he is. But the deadly fruit you have yielded recently shows the kind of trees you are: trees planted in the soil of pride, the output of love of self, which steals from you the light of reason. (L, 310)

Before the schism, in most of her letters to civil authorities Catherine had reminded them of the respect and love due to the Church because of its dignity and because of the precious gifts we are given through its ministry. Now Urban's legitimacy and the consequent duty to stay with him became her leitmotiv. She also insisted that her religious friends and disciples should comply with his request to come to Rome and help him fight for the welfare of the Church. But response was scant. She turned to prayer and sacrifice: every morning from her lodging near the Dominican church of Santa Maria sopra Minerva she went to St Peter's, and in the basilica over the tomb of the first vicar of Christ she stayed all day long, praying and fasting, 'without a single drop of water'. Under the stress of sorrow and penance her strong constitution rapidly declined: to see her on her way, she wrote to Raymond of Capua, one might think that he saw a corpse walking. Although everything seemed to go astray, still Catherine could not lose her faith in the Church: she had been told that the bridge Christ has offered mankind to reach the house of the Father cannot wholly crumble since it rests on the power of the Father, the wisdom of the Son and the 'strong hand' of the gentle Spirit of love that holds the universe. No wonder, then, if, in spite of the uneasy situation of the Church, she could see that the Bride of Christ gave life, because she has such life in herself as cannot be taken from her by anybody; that she gave strength and light so that nobody can weaken or darken her in herself. And she saw that, far from failing, her fruit is ever increasing.

Then, over the Lord's complaint about those who seek from the Church nothing but worldly advantages, her anxious appeal:

'What can I do, ineffable fire?' And he kindly answered: 'Offer your life over again, and never seek rest. This is what I have set you to do, you and those who are following and will follow you. Be careful then, never to slacken your desires and always to increase them. I never cease to be careful in providing you with my grace in your bodies and souls. . . . Aim your life and heart and affection at this bride, for me, and forget yourself.' (L, 371)

More than once Catherine had been told that renewal of the Church would not be effected by 'knife, war or cruelty', but in peace, true, humble and insistent prayer and the labours and sufferings of God's servants (cf. D, XV). This is why on her deathbed she could say to her followers: 'Be assured that I am suffering martyrdom for the Church, which is for me a cause of great rejoicing.'[6] Suffering is, in fact, the test of love, and all that Catherine was enduring for the Church was simply the result of her love for Christ. Love springs from knowledge and breeds pain, which it enjoys as a sure witness to its own identity, and also as a new opening of the mind to the mystery of life, leading to a further increase of love. Catherine had personal experience of such an interaction and this is why in the painful stress of the rising schism she could say:

Thanks, thanks be given to most high eternal God who placed us on the battlefield to fight like good knights for his bride with the shield of most holy faith. . . . The battlefield remained in our power by that virtue and might which defeated the devil and snatched humankind from its grasp. (L, 371)

Christ's weapon for the rescue of humankind was his divine love; our own love will prove the only efficient remedy to restore perfect beauty to the Bride of Christ. Love opened Catherine's mind to this truth; love sprouting from knowledge in the sunlight of faith made of Catherine the brave knight who refuses to surrender and gladly dies on the battlefield.

Notes

1. Here the *Dialogue* presents a striking similarity to St Paul's comment (Eph 4:8–14) on Psalm 68:18, 'ascending on high he took captivity as his own captive, gave gifts to men'. 'What does it mean, except that he had first descended to the lower regions of the earth?' – Yes, says Catherine – by his incarnation he descended to the level of our lowliness, and made a bridge of himself for us to ascend to the Father in Heaven. St Paul's list of those whom, on his ascension, Christ gifted with particular qualities to perform special tasks as 'apostles, prophets, evangelists, pastors and teachers' has its parallel in the passage from the *Dialogue* just quoted. Both here and in Ephesians we are told that they are so gifted that they may 'build up the body of Christ' which is the Church; so that we may 'come to unity in our faith and knowledge of the Son of God until we become the perfect Man, fully mature with the fullness of Christ himself', which is the goal to be attained by the ascent of the bridge. And, since the bridge is his doctrine, our going along it will prevent us from being 'tossed one way or another and carried away by every wind of doctrine'. The quotation from Psalm 68 follows the Vulgate version and, of course, differs from modern translations which neither Paul nor Catherine could foresee.
2. It must be noted that by 'mystical body' Catherine means the clergy, while 'universal body' indicates all those who make the body of Christ, either actually, through faith and baptism, or virtually, the way of the bridge being open to the whole of mankind. The universality of the call to salvation was emphasized in Catherine's mind by a vision: she saw Christians and infidels enter the side of Christ through the wound of the lance; then she was given a cross on her shoulders and an olive branch in her hand, and was told to take them to both peoples. Cf. L, 219.
3. The principle that members of the clergy should not be prosecuted by lay courts of justice was generally accepted in Catherine's time, and this should have challenged Church authorities on their own duty to punish unworthy priests.
4. Cf. Mark 8:33.
5. The name Clement, assumed by the antipope, must have sounded like an outrageous mockery to Italian ears because, when papal legate, Robert of Geneva had carried out bloody repressions in Cesena and other cities of central Italy.
6. Cf. *Life*, 363.

7

Catherine and politics

> I do not see how we can rule
> anybody unless we start by ruling
> ourselves. (L, 358)

Special attention has been given in recent years to Catherine's 'politics'. Even when proclaiming her a Doctor of the Church, Pope Paul VI posed the question as to whether she should be considered a politician, and his answer was yes, without doubt, but in an exceptional, thoroughly spiritual way. And this is why, he stated, 'the teaching of this singular woman politician is still meaningful and valuable'. Her politics, he said, can be summed up in her sentence:

> No state can keep in good grace with civil and divine law without holy justice. (D, CXIX)

Catherine was surprisingly aware of worldly events, and of the world being troubled. Eastern Europe was under the threat of Muslim invasion, while in its western lands the Hundred Years War offered the sad sight of two Christian nations fighting one another. When turning her attention to home business she could not help noticing discord between city and city, or among citizens of the same city, because of petty family or party rivalries. Could there be any remedy to put a stop to war and pacify such a troubled world?

It is not surprising that, while staying in Siena, Catherine should know what was going on all over Europe. Commercial traffic was frequent in her time. Italian merchants would go as far as Flanders or other northern countries and purchase coarse cloth to be finished (Catherine's father was a cloth-finisher). It is more remarkable that from a knowledge of the facts she was able to go back to the causes of the general disease, to think of remedies, and to propose them to authorities.

Her plan for peace is neatly expressed in a letter to Pope Gregory XI. She wants him to be a promoter of peace by a threefold action: to restore the papal seat to Rome, to reform the Church by purifying the clergy and to proclaim a Crusade aimed at the deliverance of the Holy Land. Apart from the possible spiritual advantages, Catherine thought that the Crusade would be of help both to put a stop to the Muslim invasion from the East, and to relieve western Europe from war by turning the interests of mercenary soldiers to a nobler aim than helping the English and the French to fight one another. Common sense told her that such men could not be expected to do anything but fighting, never having learnt to do anything else.

Besides having general information about European events, Catherine soon became practically involved in politics. Some of her friends or disciples were active in that field, and their number increased when she began to go outside the walls of Siena, first to Florence, then to Pisa and Lucca, where her presence had a specific diplomatic motivation: it had been sought to prevent the two cities from joining Tuscan states in an antipapal league. Her embassy in Avignon in favour of the Florentine rebels failed because of a change in the government of Florence, which told her something about the reliability of men in authority. There, in the 'City of the Popes', she gained an insight into the subtle ruses of French diplomats and politicians who did their best to put obstacles in her way, going so far as to try to have her sentenced under a charge of heresy. After his return to Rome, Gregory XI entrusted to Catherine the reconciliation of the Florentine republic with the Holy See, an embassy which engaged her for quite a few months and almost caused her death in a riot.

Such diplomatic activity offered to Catherine direct contact with politicians and personal knowledge of their virtues and vices, together with an understanding of the impact that individual qualities can have on the welfare of the people. They could not but strengthen her personal conviction – had there been any need for it – that what really matters for human society is the quality of its members. Personal experience was, no doubt, the basis for her ideas about good government leading to peaceful welfare. Such experience, as set in the perspective of fundamental principles, is the hallmark of her 'politics'. Catherine does not show preference for any particular system of government: a monarchy can be as good or as bad as a republic, and likewise any specific system of democratic ruling can be better or worse than another. What matters is the quality of the men in government. Just as in her desire for a renewal of the Church, Catherine strives for better quality in churchmen without bothering about structures, so, and even more, does she insist on moral reliability for civil authorities. In fact, while Church hierarchy makes the men at its higher levels, such as bishops or the Pope, responsible for the behaviour of priests – hence Catherine's persistent appeals to Pope and bishops to make use of their authority to instigate a badly needed reform of clergy behaviour – no such help is to be found at the lay level. Dante's idea of an imperial authority securing peace and welfare had faded away, and the many little city-states in Italy were far from admitting the idea of a foreign emperor meddling with their own business. Nor would his authority be acceptable to the states beyond the Alps, just then growing to consciousness of their identity and power. Therefore, for an improvement of civil welfare Catherine could only appeal personally to the men in authority. And this is what she did. Still in her early twenties, she wrote to Bernabò Visconti, the stern lord of Milan, and reminded him of the inconsistency of temporal power, the power of which he made such boast:

> No lordship we may have in this world can make us think that we are lords. I do not understand what kind of lordship that may be which can be taken from me and which does not stay within my free choice to keep. It does not seem to me that anyone should call himself lord and believe he is, being rather a steward, and a temporary one, not lasting: just as long as it will please our sweet Lord.

There is, however, a worthier lordship that we should strive for, and Catherine does not fail to call Bernabò's attention to it:

> Now, should you ask: 'Does not man have any lordship in this life?' I would answer: 'Yes, he does and it is the sweetest and gentlest, and strongest that can be had, and that is the city of our soul. Is there anything greater than to have a city where God, the supreme good, has his rest; where peace, quiet, and all sorts

of comfort are to be found? This city is so strong and its lordship
so perfect, that nobody can steal it from you, unless you consent.'

Then she insists:

> Many will conquer cities and strongholds but, having taken no
> hold of their real enemies, the world, the flesh and the devil, they
> can be said to have nothing. (L, 28)

Every human being's first experience of human society is
normally that of a family. Catherine's family was a large one,
and we can be sure that Iacopo and Lapa made good use of their
authority. Catherine certainly did not object to it, but was conscious
at the same time that it was not unbounded, as she proved by
refusing the suggestions of marriage. But she was truly fond of her
parents, as attested by her offer to endure a painful lifelong ache
to free Iacopo from Purgatory and by her reproach to one of her
brothers who caused Lapa to be anxious about him for lack of news:

> I would not like you to be unmindful of the debt you have to
> your mother, which binds you by God's commandment. I have
> seen your ingratitude grow to the point that, let alone giving
> her support – from which you are excused, because I know you
> could not do so – even of words you have been sparing. In your
> ingratitude you have not considered her labour in giving you
> birth and the milk she gave you from her breast, and how she
> toiled in rearing you and the others. (L, 18)

Catherine does not think that the relationship between mother
and children should stop at the material, biological level. She writes
to Lapa, who had grown a little nervous both about her protracted
absence and about the gossip among the good wives in Siena:

> With great desire have I wished to see in you a true mother, not
> just of my body but also of my soul. (L, 240)

What could she mean by wishing Lapa to prove a true mother of
her soul if not that she would understand and accept her daughter's
extraordinary mission? This mission implied the risk of misunderstanding and criticism, but it would turn to an increase of
merit for her soul, and this should be a motive for rejoicing, rather
than for complaining:

> If you love my soul better than my body, any undue fondness of
> yours will die, and my bodily absence will not be so hard to bear;

it will rather be of comfort to you . . . My working towards the honour of God is not without an increase in grace and virtue in my soul. It is true, then, that if you, sweetest mother, come to love my soul better than my body, you will be comforted, not discomforted. (Ibid.)

The role of parents is one that requires a good deal of self-denial. No doubt they may expect some return for their efforts in raising their children, but probably not according to their plans. God lhas his own unforeseen plans for human beings and their variety should cause us to rejoice in seeing the boundless ways of his love. He lends everybody talents, which parents will have to foster and help to grow to full maturity, without any prospect of personal advantage. This is what Catherine tries to explain to Stefano Maconi's mother who, like Lapa, was worrying about the absence of her son:

Suppose you asked: 'How am I to love?', I would answer that children and everything else should be loved for the sake of their Creator, not selfishly . . . not in view of any advantage or as if they were your own property, but as something given you on loan. Whatever is given to us in this life is given to be made use of as a loan, and is left to us as long as it pleases divine Goodness, the giver. Behave as one whose duty it is to distribute all things in the name of Christ crucified, both as regards material wealth, by helping the poor as far as you can, and your children, whose needs you must supply and whom you must nourish and raise in the respect of God: you should prefer them to die rather than offend God. And, were you to see that God is calling them, do not oppose his sweet will, and if they are willing to give one hand, you, for your part, give both. Do not pretend to choose their stations in life according to your own views – to do so would mean that your love for them is separate from God's love – but be pleased with whatever situation God calls them to. (L, 247)

Simple-minded mothers, who love their children according to worldly standards, will try to resist God's call and keep their children for themselves and thus completely lose them. And it is right it should be so, since they prove so ignorant and proud as to claim 'to impose on the Holy Spirit who is calling them'.

To another noble lady she wrote:

Let us take from our heart any disorderly love, of children, of husband, of wealth. Keep them and love them as things lent, since everything is given us on loan that we may make use of it. Let them last as long as pleases God, who gave them to you. It is unfair to possess what is not ours as if it were. (L, 90)

Since in Catherine's plan for good government particular stress is laid on the moral qualities of the men in government, it is quite natural that she should insist on sound education for the sons and daughters of her married friends. All evils afflicting human society have their roots deep in the hearts of men and women, and can be summed up in unruly attachment to gain and ambition of power; this is why Catherine insists on spurning worldly pleasures and advantages. She advises one of her friends, a man of rather high status, to get rid of superfluous furniture and luxurious clothing. Both are harmful because

they infatuate the heart and foster pride by causing one to feel above others, and to make boast of what he should not. We, false Christians should be ashamed to enjoy such commodities while our Head is tormented . . . Clothe yourself in a normal, convenient, not too expensive way, and God will be pleased with you. And, as far as it depends on your authority, see that your wife and children do likewise, so that you may be rule and doctrine to them; as a father should be who has to rear his children by reason and virtuous doings. And, besides, use marriage with the reverence due to the sacrament . . . as a reasonable man, not like a brute. Then you and she will be the good trees that yield good fruit. (L, 258)

Love of justice is seen by Catherine as the essential virtue for a man of government, but to exert it with regard to his subjects he must have practised it on himself, with detachment from selfish views and interests. This is what Catherine explains to Joanna, Queen of Naples, well known to be anything but a model of virtue:

Keep in mind that you have before you a twofold way to exert justice. First on yourself, by acknowledging that you owe to God whatever you have, thus rendering glory and honour to him, while sin and misery are your own . . . The other justice is to be done to human creatures, and this one you have to keep in your kingdom. I therefore beg you in Christ Jesus not to turn your eyes away from injustice, but to see that, according to justice, everybody, whether important or not, is given his due. And be careful not to let desire to please, or fear of anybody, prevent your doing so. (L, 133)

To her follower Andrea di Vanni, who had at the time a role in the government of Siena as 'Captain of the People', Catherine insists on the urgency of acquiring virtues and, first of all, justice, if he wants to prove a good administrator:

> Dearest child in Christ the sweet Jesus, . . . I am writing to you in his precious blood, desiring to see in you a rightful and good administrator, so that the honour of God and your desire, a good one that God gave you in his mercy, may be fulfilled. But I do not see how we can ever rule other people unless we start by ruling ourselves. When someone rules himself, he rules the others in the same way, because he loves his neighbours by the same love he has for himself. Just as God's perfect charity breeds love of neighbours, so will one rule his subjects as perfectly as he rules himself. (L, 358)

To govern is, then, seen as an act of love. Its aim is to bring about at the level of civil society the good of the law of love that binds all human beings. And, just as right love of self implies the effort to make the most of one's talents, so does authority afford the possibility of working towards a better use of these talents for the welfare of the community.

> Whatever holy justice dictates proceeds from the order that one has rightly set and observed in the three powers of his soul. Having it in himself, he shares it with his neighbours by means of prayer, speech and the example of good and saintly behaviour. And if a man has to govern, as well as observing the law himself, he wants to have it observed by his subjects, and to have it observed, he punishes transgressors out of love for justice . . . And according to the rule of justice, he imposes slight or great [punishment] as reason requires. (L, 358)

Justice should never yield either to allurements or to threats: a righteous man would keep it at all costs, and so avoid the many evils which come from lack of it.

On the primary importance of justice Catherine writes to Ser Andreasso Cavalcabuoi, then a member of the government in Siena. Her desire is to find in him a righteous lord, which means that in his lordship he should be a defender of justice, according to reason, never permitting anybody's influence to weigh on him when passing judgement. This supposes the presence of the virtue of justice in the judge. Without it, he will have no concern except about how to take advantage of his position and satisfy his own pleasure. The likeness Catherine sketches of the self-centred governor may have been suggested by personal experience:

> He is cruel, since, out of greed for money or under undue influence, he may be made a devourer of his neighbours' flesh. We often see that such men only maintain justice against the poor – which may often be sheer injustice – but do not so exercise it over the great, the powerful. This comes from love of self and too high a self-esteem. Such a man is unjust and therefore he cannot maintain holy and true justice. He has no consideration for the city of his soul; his only concern is for his miserable body which he seeks to please by spending all his time in lust, pride, luxury, vanity, all of which are deadly to him. As for his miserable soul, which should be God's temple where he can rest by his grace, he has made of it the devil's abode, and has caused this noble city [his soul] to surrender to the nothingness of sin. He is like one blinded and deprived of reason, unmindful of the harm to himself ... Having no care for his own city, he will never have any care for the city in his lordship, and instead of working towards the general welfare, he will only be mindful of his own pleasure or advantage. (L, 338)

Justice is undoubtedly Catherine's favourite topic when dealing with men in authority. She insists on it in dealing with the 'Magnificent Lord Defenders of the People' in Siena. She wants them to have 'the pearl of justice' shining on their breasts by overcoming their love of self and attending to the universal welfare of the city: the self-centred have little or no regard for justice, and in exchange for the promise of money or of unlawful help they will refrain from punishing those who have earned severe censure. Such behaviour is perverse, and the judge should be given the punishment from which he freed the criminal who paid to be declared not guilty.

> This is a wicked man's doing, and he ought to be given the same punishment which the criminal he freed for money had earned. And such a man would pass merciless sentence on poor harmless people whose guilt may not even reach one thousandth of that man's fault. The miserable man, who has been set to govern the city while he does not even govern himself, will pretend not to know that poor women and men are being robbed and, far from being of help to them in their suits, he will be careful that the offender is declared not guilty. I am not surprised that

they are unjust, when they prove so cruel to themselves in living indecently, wallowing in dirty mud at almost swinish level, and so proudly that their pride will not suffer them to be told the truth. They bite their neighbours by reproaches, by unlawful profits and endless other evil doings I do not name to avoid annoying you by too many words. I do not wonder, then, that they are lacking in holy and true justice and this is why God has allowed and allows us to be given such punishments and scourges as seem to me not to have had any equal since the beginning of the world. (L, 367)

The results of a trial are largely dependent on lawyers, and the great problem for the poor is how to obtain their help when they have no money to pay for it. Appeals in their favour are to be found here and there in Catherine's letters. When writing to Lorenzo del Pino, a doctor of law in Bologna, she starts by reminding him that truth, complete truth, should never be concealed. 'I want to see you', she says, 'a lover and follower of truth and spurner of falsehood.'

To become lovers and followers of truth we have to look at Christ crucified, the revealer of supreme truth, God's infinite love for all of us. The man who fails to understand that such love binds us to a return of love to our neighbours will neglect his duty for worldly advantages:

He feeds on miserable worldly things and, whatever his position, he corrupts himself, so that if he has an office involving a duty to do something for his neighbours, he does not comply, except as far as he can find his own profit in that service, and no further. He is a lover of himself. Christ, our blessed Lord, gave his life for us, and he is unwilling to say one word on behalf of his neighbour unless he can expect to be paid and overpaid. Suppose the suitor is poor and cannot afford paying, he will keep him in suspense before telling him the truth; and more than once he may even not do so at all and will just make fun of him. Instead of proving to the poor a merciful father, as he should, he turns cruel to his own soul by offending them. But the miserable man does not realize that the supreme Judge will return to him nothing but what he has given, since rightfully every sin shall be punished and every good deed rewarded. (L, 193)

Now, Lorenzo was a distinguished person, was married, was wealthy: could he save his soul in spite of all that? Catherine has no doubt:

O dearest brother, whatever a man's position, he can save his soul and receive the life of grace . . . every position is pleasant to God; he has no preference: only holy desire is acceptable to him. We may, therefore, keep our property, provided our attachment to it is orderly . . . We can see that the slaves of the world, the lovers of falsehood, have to bear great sufferings in their lifetime and in the end cruel torments. Why? Because of their disorderly fondness for themselves and for created beings which they love apart from God. This is why divine Goodness has disposed that every disorderly affection should prove unbearable to itself.

Falsehood is a cheater of its lovers: while someone believes that he has hold of what he is so fond of, he will find himself deprived of everything.

You see, then, that all things are transitory, so that we should keep them in a rational way, and in the light of reason . . . Such a tree will prove a fruitful one, producing the fruit of virtue, and though it remains in the midst of stinking corruption, will give fragrance, and its seed will be good and virtuous. (L, 193)

No position, however important, can deprive us of God's friend-ship, provided we are careful to make our sound foundation on charity. This is what Catherine recommends to the King of Hungary. Charity frees the soul from resentment for personal offences and makes it benevolent to the offender, which will amount to turning his soul from hatred to love, or 'heaping red-hot coals on his head' (Rom 12:20). The presence of charity in the soul is tested by the patient bearing of personal injury, great or small, and by generous service to fellow beings in their need. A king, for all his power, is not exempt from the law of charity: it binds him as it binds the least of his subjects. He should enjoy having a wider field open to his good will. Benevolent overcoming of personal resentment is the right condition for a righteous judge to give everyone his due

to the great and the small, to the poor as to the wealthy. He does not contaminate justice because of any allurement or threat, either to please or displease: he keeps the scales level and gives each one according to reason. (L, 357)

To keep the scales level, never allowing influence to weigh on either side, requires courage and implies responsibility. If every person has to feel responsible for the impact of his own behaviour on society, all the more should those who have been given authority over common welfare. Lordship is not just a title to be honoured, it is a challenge to work. As Catherine says to Pope Gregory XI:

> Since God has given you authority, and you have accepted it, you have to make use of your privileges and power; if you are unwilling to do so, it would be better for you to renounce what you [once] accepted. (L, 255)

Catherine stresses this point when addressing authorities. Rulers and politicians cannot be allowed to lie asleep in 'the bed of neglect' while enemies are besieging the city or spreading discord within its walls; they must keep their eyes wide open and react, as does 'the dog of conscience' that barks as soon as he senses an enemy approaching.

Courage and manly fortitude are most necessary in men in government, not only for facing possible enemies, but especially for them to be credible and reliable:

> I want you to be constant and persevering in virtue, unlike the leaf that turns in the breeze. (L, 363)

Catherine had personal experience of such inconstancy in the behaviour of the Florentine politicians, hence her reproach:

> Nothing but shame and confusion would come from your giving one promise, and behaving in the opposite way. (L, 230)

In fact, after professing repentance for their rebellion and entrusting Catherine with the task of reconciliation, they had imposed new taxes on the clergy, which meant that their repentance was not so sincere as they had pretended. Such ambiguous behaviour, she says, is an offence to God and no help towards peacemaking.

Similar duplicity was a source of complaint in the behaviour of the ambassadors that Florence sent to Avignon; it proved that their request to Catherine to plead the cause of the Republic with the Pope lacked sincerity:

> I am being made aware that [your] humble words came from fear and need, rather than from love or virtuous desire. In fact, had the fault been sincerely acknowledged, your deeds would have been in tune with the sound of your words. (L, 234)

Catherine's reproach to Joanna of Naples for her inconstancy is no less severe for its being mingled with warm expressions of love:

You are behaving like one who is the prey of passion . . . you are not aware of the sentence that will be passed on you. Alas, my heart aches as I say these words, because I so tenderly desire your salvation. . . . Neither wealth nor your great kingdom with its nobility and common people, your physical subjects, will have an opportunity to plead for you with the supreme Judge. . . . You have caused, and are still causing, all your subjects to stand against you rather than for you, since they have found so little truth in your person; not the condition of a man with a manly heart, but that of a female lacking firmness and stability: a leaf turning in the wind in a feminine way. (L, 317)[1]

To keep true to one's given word may require quite a lot of manly courage, but rulers and politicians *have* to be courageous: lack of courage would make them the slaves of servile fear.

The man whose soul fears in a servile way fails to perfect whatever he does, either of great or small matter. How dangerous such fear is! It cuts off the arms of desire. (L, 242)

Having its arms cut off, desire ceases to be the driving power leading to action; it is reduced to a vague, useless wishing.

O love of self and servile fear, you blind the mind's eye, you prevent its coming to see the truth. You take away the life of grace, together with lordship over one's own city, and over the city on loan. You make a man unbearable to himself, because he is made to want what he cannot have, while possession of what he has is painful, because he fears he may lose it. So by always vacillating between desire and fear, he has a real foretaste of hell in his lifetime. (L, 123)

Servile fear hinders justice and leads to unjust sentencing, as in the trial of the Lord Jesus Christ:

Truly, dearest brothers, this is the perverse fear and love that killed Christ, because Pilate was blinded by his fear of losing lordship and did not know Truth, and this is why he killed Christ. Nevertheless, what he was dreading befell him because afterwards, when it pleased God – not that he was pleased with that fault – he lost soul and body and lordship . . . I feel as if the whole world were filled with such Pilates who, out of blind fear, do not mind persecuting God's servants. (Ibid.)

This letter, addressed to the Lord Defenders of the city of Siena, develops and gives a full description of what Catherine means by 'a city on loan', an original phrase of hers. After calling their attention to the dangers of slavish fear, she presents the advantages of holy fear that will give the rulers lordship in their own personal city and on the city on loan: a lordship never to be stolen by man or devil.

Our own city is the city of our soul, which we possess with holy fear founded on brotherly charity, peace and union with God and neighbours, and sound, true virtues. Should someone live in hatred and grudging and discord, full of selfish love and impurity . . . he would not have it in his power.

Such a man has no hold on his city; he is under the sway of his vices and sins, and has so abased himself as to permit the thing that is not (sin) to master him, thus losing the dignity that [divine] grace gave him. He despises the blood of Christ, the price that was paid for us, and that makes us know divine mercy and supreme eternal Truth, ineffable Love, who created us and rescued us by blood, not by gold or silver, and disclosed to us how great and noble our soul is. One must be truly blind, then, not to see such a fire of love, and the great misery he comes to by lying in the darkness of mortal sin and having no lordship over himself, as I already said. He can hardly have lordship over what is being lent to him unless he has started by ruling himself.

Lordships on loan are cities and other temporary dominions which are lent to us and to others all over the world for a given lapse of time, according to the pleasure of divine bounty, and after local ways and customs so that, either by death or even during our lifetime, they come to an end. They prove, at any rate, that they are on loan.

The man who has lordship over himself will keep them with holy fear and ordered, not disordered, love, as something given on loan, not as if it were his own property. He will consider the lordship entrusted to him with fear of and respect for the entruster. By nobody but God were you given it. Therefore, when we are asked to return the loan, we should do so without risking eternal death. I want you, then, to govern with holy, true fear. I tell you that there is no other way to keep both spiritual and temporal positions except to live virtuously, since both never fail except as a result of our sins and faults. Remove sin, and fear will be removed; your heart will be strong, not timid, and you shall not be afraid of your own shadow. (Ibid.)

Catherine's constant paralleling of the two cities, our own soul and the political body whose members we are and over which we may have to exert lordship, brings us back to the very foundation of her doctrine, the basic teaching she was imparted about God's fullness of being and our nothingness that owes to him 'being and whatever is added to being'. In this light we are led to realize that our personal qualities are lent to us not to be buried in the ground, but to be traded and increased, as in the parable of the talents: every single person has to respond to the talents he or she has been lent. From the individual, the idea of the loan extends to family: husband, wife, children as well as property are on loan and must be used within God's plan. A further extension of the same principle leads to good lordship over a city and also to good and peaceful understanding among states and nations.

The principle that the welfare of the city relies on the qualities of its citizens implies that rulers and politicians must be aware of the rights of their subjects at all levels. Not that they might be expected to become spiritual leaders, but while providing for order and peace and material welfare, they should not forget that their subjects are made of body and soul, and must not be asked to do anything against their consciences. This is firmly stated in a letter reproaching Joanna of Naples for her allegiance to Clement, the antipope: by doing so she was dividing her subjects into rival parties and made her followers rebels against the Church.

Alas, dearest mother! ... If you are not careful of your own salvation, be mindful of the peoples entrusted to your hands: your subjects, whom you ruled diligently and peacefully for so long. Now, because of your actions against truth, you see them in such disunion, war and murders, behaving like animals because of that confounded division. Alas, how can your heart avoid bursting and allow them to be divided because of you, so that one is made a follower of the white, and the other of the red rose; one goes after truth while the other seeks falsehood? Alas, for my unhappy soul! Do you not see that all of them were created by the purest rose, God's will, and created anew to grace by that most ardent rose, the blood of Christ ... which gathered us in the garden of holy Church? ...

Do you not see that you are being cruel to yourself? In fact their evils and divisions lessen your authority. And besides, you will have to give an account to God for the souls that you are causing to perish. How will you? Very badly. (L, 362)[2]

Unity and peace within the walls of a city or the boundaries of a state as well as among nations should be considered by politicians as of first importance, because they are much more vital for the welfare of the people than power and other material advantages. When asking Charles V of France to make peace with the King of England, his 'brother' since they share the same Christian faith, Catherine first calls his attention to the basic principles that should inspire our behaviour, 'God's sweet commandments': unless we comply with them and imitate the 'sweet Lamb', Christ, we cannot have a share in his redeeming blood. Upon this she makes a three-fold request to King Charles: that he should spurn worldly and selfish interests, keep justice and be careful that it be well kept all over his kingdom, put a stop to the war and turn hatred into love. He should understand the teaching that our Master gave us from his cross:

> What my soul most wishes to see in you is love of your neigh-bours with whom you have been at war so long . . . First sweet Truth . . . gave you his example while hanging from the wood of the most holy cross. While the Jews are shouting: 'Crucify him!' he exclaims in humble and mild voice: 'Father, forgive them, they do not know what they are doing' (Luke 23:20, 34). Consider his inestimable charity: not only does he pardon, he apologizes for them to the Father. (L, 235)

The other way, the way of hatred, leads to harm to body and soul:

> One must be a blind fool not to see that with the knife of hatred he is killing himself.

But it is not just a matter of personal harm: war weighs so heavily on the people that one should be careful to avoid it at all costs. Catherine persists with Charles:

> Do not mind losing worldly dominions: loss will turn into gain, provided you make your soul at peace with your brother. I wonder how you can help committing to this aim not only material goods, but your very life, if possible, on considering what harm there has been to souls and bodies, and how many religious, women, girls, have been abused and persecuted because of this war. No more [of it], for the sake of Christ crucified! (Ibid.)

Though peace should be sought with great effort, fighting cannot be avoided in particular instances when, we might say, truth is at stake. Such was the situation in the spring of 1379 when Clement, then in Avignon, made an effort to conquer the city of Rome, where a detachment of his soldiers was already stationed in the fortress of Castel Sant'Angelo. Had he succeeded, Urban, the true Pope, would not have been spared, and the false one might have found more followers. Clement's Breton soldiers had to be opposed: the Italian Company of St George fought and defeated Clement's men, which resulted in the surrender of the garrison in the fortress.

Catherine had words of praise for the Company and wise advice for its captain, Alberico da Barbiano:

> Who is the Lord for whose sake you have entered the battlefield? It is Christ crucified, supreme, eternal Good. . . . O dearest brother and sons, you are knights entering the battlefield to give your life for the sake of life, and your blood for the sake of the blood of Christ crucified. This is a time for new martyrs. You are the first to give your blood. What is the fruit you are to receive for it? Eternal life, an infinite fruit. . . . Do you want to be so strong that each one shall be as good as many? Suggest to your mind's eye the blood of sweet, kind Jesus, the humble Lamb, and our faith which, as you see, is being contaminated by the wicked lovers of self, who deny that Urban VI is the true Pope, a truth they first told us.

Then follows advice: the men in the Company should have a pure conscience, free of mortal sin; they should not aim at acquiring riches: one cannot, at the same time, both plunder and fight. Alberico is advised to choose, as officers, manly and reliable men and to beware of traitors, either inside or outside his Company. The theme of truth newly emerges as Catherine proposes devotion to the Blessed Virgin as a sure defence against treason:

> I want you and the others to offer yourselves . . . to Mary, the sweet mother, and pray her to be your advocate and defender and, for the sake of the sweet loving Word she bore in her womb, never to suffer you to be deceived in any way, and make you aware of any attempt to deceive you, so that deceit may not lead you to perish.

Then a promise of help, through her prayers:

We shall do as Moses did: while people were fighting, he prayed, and as long as he prayed, people were winning. This is what we will do, hoping our prayer may be acceptable. (L, 347)[3]

After the deliverance of Rome from the threat of invasion Catherine wrote to the civil authorities of the city to remind them of the debt of gratitude they owed to the soldiers who had exposed their lives for its sake. By doing so she pointed out that this virtue is not at all unbecoming in men at government: 'I am writing to you, wishing to see you grateful for the many blessings you have been given.' Ingratitude 'dries up the fountain of piety' within the soul and fosters all sorts of vicious habits, such as pride, inconstancy, hatred, envy, selfishness, injustice, which press so badly on the heart as to leave no room for God or neighbour. By ingratitude we are led to forget that speech is granted so that we may give praise to God, not for us to indulge in criticizing and slandering. Gratitude, by contrast, has a clearly positive impact on the human soul. On these grounds Catherine focuses the present situation and its appeals to gratitude:

I want you, dearest brothers, to be grateful for the favours granted by our Creator, so that they may be increased. Those you were given lately were almost miraculous, and I want you to render thanks and praise to his name, since you must acknowledge, with sincere humility, that you owe them to God, not to your own power and skill: all your human endeavours would not have done what God did. He turned the eye of his mercy to us in our great danger, and to him we have to ascribe them. (L, 349)

However, God's mercy made use of the men in the Company; they fought at the risk of their own lives and acquired a right to the gratitude of the people they freed from threat of invasion and violence:

I also want you to be grateful to this Company who were Christ's instruments, and help them in their need, and, above all, the men who were badly wounded. Behave charitably and peacefully with them, so that they may stay on your side, and have no motive to turn against you. This is what you had better do, dearest brothers, both because of their due and of your great need.

Catherine knows that a reminder of the practical situation can make politicians more sensitive to spiritual or moral motives. And after praising the quality of gratitude, she does not spare them reproach for their ingratitude:

> I feel as if you were ungrateful to Giovanni Cenci, who strove to free you from the scourge you had from Castel Sant'Angelo. He behaved with great concern and loyalty and a true heart, only to please God and be of help to us with no concern for himself, as I well know. Now, far from showing him any token of gratitude or giving him thanks, envy and ingratitude are throwing at him the poison of slander and backbiting. I would not like you to do so either to him or to anybody who might be doing service to you: that would mean offence to God and harm to you, since the whole community is in need of wise men, mature and prudent and upright. No more, for the sake of Christ crucified! Stop it as you think best, and do not allow the simplicity of the ignorant to prevent what is good for you. This I say for your own good and not out of any passion of mine – you know I am a pilgrim here – and I am speaking for your welfare, because I hold you all, together with him, as if you were my own soul. (Ibid.)

When declaring her love for the people in Rome, Catherine was simply asserting the leading principle of all her political or diplomatic activity. Love for the whole of mankind made her alert to the threats to common welfare all over Europe and caused her appeals to the rulers of European states. Love had kept her constant to the mission in Florence, with which Pope Gregory had entrusted her; love, tested and increased by long endurance, burst forth in her words announcing the arrival of the olive branch, the sign of peace restored:

> O dearest children, God has listened to the cry and the voice of his servants who have been appealing to him for so long, and to their loud howling over the dead children. Now they are reviving: from death they have come to life, from blindness to light. O dearest children, the lame walk, the deaf hear, blind eyes see, and the dumb speak: they joyfully shout out with powerful voices: 'Peace, peace, peace!' and heartily rejoice to find that they have come back to obedience and to their father's favour, peace being restored in their minds.

Catherine's spontaneous appropriation to the coming of peace in Florence of the events said to have marked the Redeemer's own advent[4] might seem a bit far-fetched, but it was not, since the success of her mission was spiritual rather than political:

Now do they begin to understand, and they say: 'Thanks to you, Lord, for having made peace for us with our holy Father.' Now they call holy the sweet Lamb, Christ-on-earth, whom they used to call heretic. (L, 303)

Catherine's efforts were always aimed at the spiritual welfare of the people on whose behalf she was working, which explains how she could so devote herself to the cause of Florence, Siena's traditional rival. Her desire for the welfare of all human creatures could not be bounded within the walls of one city, all the more so as she was well aware of how much misunderstanding, hatred and fighting was produced by the fragmentation of Italy into small states.

Her concept of her own country overcame local boundaries; she understood that, in spite of temporary political divisions, there was a natural unity binding together all the states in the peninsula, as appears in her reproach to the three Italian cardinals who had given allegiance to Clement. Why, says Catherine, not even at the barely human level can you find an excuse for your choice in the passionate love of your fatherland, as your colleagues 'beyond the mountains' do, since 'you are Italian and Christ-on-earth is Italian'. No matter whether they had been born in Milan, Florence or Rome, or in the kingdom of Naples, they were simply Italian because all of them belonged to the land south of the Alps.[5]

But Rome held a very special place in Catherine's heart because the Gospel had first been announced there by Peter and Paul, and from there had spread all over the world. It was Peter's see, and Catherine had struggled hard to bring Pope Gregory XI back to it, while now she was struggling even harder to prevent Robert of Geneva, an interloper, from usurping the title and authority of Peter's lawful successor. When walking along the streets of the city, she felt as if the blood of the martyrs of old were 'boiling' under her feet as a challenge to spend her own life for the sake of Christ crucified, and of his 'sweet Bride', the Church.[6]

Since Rome was at the time the capital of one of the small states into which Italy was fractioned, the Pope had to attend both to spiritual and political affairs and to local government. With Urban, a decidedly stern and authoritarian character, Catherine insists on the need for governors to stoop to the level of their subjects and try to catch their feelings and expectations. A wise understanding of the people's character may prove a better help for good government than stern authority and angry rebukes. Misunderstandings that had occurred in Rome between the prefect of the city and delegates of the people were quite probably to be attributed to a lack of that kind disposition in the prefect, and Catherine feels that she must warn Pope Urban:

> I heard, most holy Father, of the prefect's angry and irreverent answer to the Roman ambassadors ... upon which they are going to send you their delegates. I beg you, most holy Father, to meet them often, as you used to do, and prudently bind them [to you] with love's binding. I likewise beg you that now, when they come to you after holding their counsel, you receive them as amiably as you can ... I beg your pardon, I am probably saying what I should not, knowing that you are certainly aware of the character of your Roman children who are more easily drawn and bound by kindness, than by any other power or by harsh words. (L, 370)

When in Florence on her mission of peace, Catherine had reminded Urban that what really mattered was to restore the Florentines to Church communion, and that, in spite of their short-comings, they were not so bad, after all: he should simply try not to urge too much of them:

> I beg you, and compel you in the name of Christ crucified, for the sake of his blood whose minister you are, not to delay in receiving the sheep that have been away from the fold; let your kind holiness win their hardness, and grant them the privilege of being restored to the fold. And, suppose they are not asking for it with such true and perfect humility as they should, let your holiness supply their imperfection and bring it to perfection. Accept from the sick what they can give. . . . Your children are seeking from you the ointment of mercy, and even though they are not asking for it as politely as one might wish . . . do not give up, because they will prove better children than others. (L, 291)

Kind words should never form a pleasant clothing for a deceptive message. No promise should ever be made unless one can reasonably foresee that it can be fulfilled:

> I humbly beg you to be prudent, and always to take care to promise only what you will be able to accomplish fully, and so prevent harm, shame and confusion from ensuing. Pardon me, sweetest and most holy Father, for saying such words to you. I trust that your humility and kindness will be pleased with them,

and that you will not despise them because they are said by a miserable woman: a humble person does not consider who is speaking; he only cares for God's honour, truth and his own welfare. (Ibid.)

All advisers are not necessarily trustworthy, but when advice is given by the 'miserable woman' whose name is Catherine there is no risk in listening to it:

A loving child cannot bear that anything be done to the injury or shame of his father; he is well aware that a father who has to govern a large family cannot see more than a single man does; this is why, unless his children were careful of their father's honour and welfare, he might often be cheated. You are father and lord of the universal body of the Christian religion, we are, all of us, under the wings of your Holiness; your authority is boundless, but your insight is just that of one man. It is up to your children, then, to see and provide, with sincere hearts void of servile fear, for God's honour and your own honour and welfare, including the welfare of the sheep in your care. I know that your Holiness earnestly desires to have helpers that may be of help, but you should be patient and listen to them. (L, 302)

Rulers should be careful not to believe charges laid about this or that without first ascertaining what kind of person the one who speaks is and of whom he is speaking: backbiting can be just as useful as praise to further personal aims. Urban should be particularly careful when candidates for Church offices are introduced to him: he should make sure that they want to serve God and their neighbours and are not aiming at the material advantages connected with prelatures, and that the person who proposes a candidate is not expecting personal advancement from the other's promotion to office.

The task of an adviser is very delicate: he should not use his familiarity with lords to foster their ambitions or, still worse, to encourage their bad habits by pretending that he shares them, which is base hypocrisy. Catherine warns a Neapolitan lady, a confidante of the queen's, against the danger of committing such a hideous crime:

Holy fear of God makes the soul manly, fearless of either suffering, or death, or persecution . . . Of this holy fear we are in need today . . . and we must avoid miserable love of self, the source of servile fear, which is so timid as to be afraid of its own shadow . . . so that, on seeing that God and neighbour are being offended, someone will pretend not to see the offence . . . moreover, to please and avoid displeasing, he will show agreement with the same crimes that are being committed, and behave against conscience . . . Dearest sister, I beg you to get rid of such servile fear, and start sowing truth in the queen's heart, in holy fear of God. (L, 361)

It is hardly possible for us to ascertain today whether and to what extent Catherine's political endeavours had any impact on the politicians, her contemporaries, but her letters prove as effective today as they were six centuries ago and politicians might still learn something from them.

In Siena City Hall, Ambrogio Lorenzetti's frescoes realistically depict the outcome of both good and bad government. Dark, cruel images of violence and murder on one wall are a clear expression of what misgovernment can lead to. The opposite wall displays a comforting vision of city and country under good government: girls are dancing in the square while a teacher is sitting in front of attentive pupils and masons are busy at work. A countryman has just come in through the open gate, his donkey laden with produce to sell, and from the same gate a company of gentlemen on horseback is moving out to the country on a hunting party; far in the distance a man is tilling the ground. Everything is peacefully alive.

Lorenzetti died when Catherine was a baby, and she may have seen his paintings. But her bent was not so much towards the description of consequences as to the research of their causes, and the causes for good or evil in human society, she knew, were to be sought in man's heart, in his reasonable, or wild, use of his own qualities.

About two centuries later William Shakespeare was to make one of his characters say: 'This above all: to thine own self be true, and it must follow, as the night the day, thou canst not then be false to any man.'[7] Did Shakespeare ever read Catherine? It is not impossible since the English translation of the *Dialogue* had long been published. At any rate, he was in perfect tune with Catherine in saying how important it is for man to be true to himself. Having been so bountifully gifted with understanding and will, and given love as his own natural law to be obeyed by free choice, man has simply to be true to himself, to the divine idea of his being.

In one of her last letters, Catherine summed up her ideas about the ideal politician in a few words: 'If you are what you ought to be, you will set all Italy afire' (L, 368). What really matters is to be; to do will be its natural result: once we have well ruled 'the city of our soul' we shall have acquired the fundamental disposition to be good rulers of 'the city on loan', at any time, in any country.

Notes

1. 'Female', 'feminine', sound scornful on Catherine's lips: they sum up characteristics she despises such as futility, instability, sensuality, emotionalism. When a woman, with manly determination, overcomes such faults, she is worth the name of *donna* meaning *domina* or 'lady' because she holds the reins of government over her own city. Queen Joanna had given a striking example of inconstancy in turning from Urban to Clement. On the former's election she had encouraged public rejoicing, which was quite natural since Urban was, by birth, a subject of the kingdom of Naples. Her shift to Clement may have been caused by dynastic interests. She belonged, in fact, to the house of Anjou which numbered among its members Charles V of France, a supporter of Clement.
2. The white rose was the sign of allegiance to Urban VI, the red rose meant adherence to Clement, the antipope.
3. The Company of St George had its great victory over the troops of the antipope on 29 April 1379, exactly one year before Catherine's death, and the victory was attributed to her prayers, because the army fighting for Clement was a large one. Cf. Exodus 17:11.
4. Cf. Matthew 11:4–5; Luke 7:22.
5. Cf. L, 310.
6. Cf. L, 329.
7. *Hamlet*, I, iii, 78–80.

8

The way to perfect love

Staying on the cross
like one in love. (L. 225)

The first petition Catherine makes in the *Dialogue* is for herself: she asks God to punish her for all the evil deeds in the world for which her own sins make her feel responsible. The petition sounds rather bold, but the answer shows that it is being accepted and why:

Then eternal Truth, by increasingly catching and drawing to himself her desire, did as he used to do in the Old Testament when, a sacrifice being offered, fire came and drew to him the sacrifice he accepted. This is how sweet Truth dealt with that soul: he sent the fire of the gentle Holy Spirit to catch the sacrifice of the desire she was making of herself and said: 'Don't you know, dear child, that all the sufferings that one bears, or might bear, in his lifetime cannot atone for the slightest sin? It is so because the offence made to me, infinite Goodness, requires infinite atonement. I want you to understand that all the sufferings given during life are not given as punishment: they are meant to amend and cure the child who has failed. In fact, atonement is made by the soul's desire, with true repentance and displeasure of sin.' (D, III).

This passage is a prelude to a theme that will be developed all through the *Dialogue* and is constantly present in Catherine's mind and writings: the different values of spirit and matter. The reference to Elijah's challenge to the prophets of Baal (1 Kings 18:20–32) is very effective in presenting the inanity of physical effort

131

on its own, and Catherine certainly did not miss the comedy in the prophets' torturing their bodies and invoking Baal louder and louder while Elijah mocks them for their ineffective efforts. Here the superiority of spirit over matter is evidenced by God's response to Elijah's desire for his honour, granting what the material worship of the prophets failed to obtain.

Suffering may help in atoning for sin, provided it is inspired by the spirit:

> True contrition atones for the offence and its punishment, not by way of the finite chastisement that one might offer, but by infinite desire; because infinite God requires infinite love and infinite sorrow. (Ibid.)

No action is good or bad in itself. Its quality depends on conformity or opposition to God's law, which is the law of love. Rebellion to the law is refusal of love, and lack of love can only be atoned for by a surplus of love. This principle is further stated:

> As you see, satisfaction is made by the soul's desire, when it is united to me, infinite Goodness, more or less, according to the perfection of love in the person who offers prayer and desire . . . Feed, then, the fire of your desire, and let no time pass without appealing to me for them by humble and continuous prayer. (D, IV)

Then Catherine is given further instruction about God's appreciation of the desire to bear suffering for the sake of one's neighbours:

> Very pleasant to me is the desire willingly to bear any trouble and labour until death for the salvation of souls. The more one bears, the better he proves that he loves me; by loving me he comes to know more about my truth, and the more he knows, the more he smarts with pain and sorrow for having been offended. You asked for suffering so that you might have the faults of others punished in you and did not realize that you were asking for love, light and knowledge of truth since, as I already told you, the wider love grows, the wider sorrow and suffering grow: sorrow increases with increase in love . . . know that the love of divine charity is so bound in the soul to perfect patience, that you cannot lose one without losing the other. This is why, when one chooses to love me, he must also choose to bear for my sake whatever trials I may grant him. Patience is never tested except in hardships, and it is joined to charity. Endure, then, in a manly way, otherwise you

would not prove faithful spouses and children of my Truth, eager for my honour and the salvation of souls. (D, V)

Suffering is an everyday companion to every man and woman: why? The answer given to Catherine is: not to punish, but to change for the better the child who has offended. By the use of the word 'child' the question turns from judicial to educational. Though atonement had been the object of Catherine's petition, she is now told that suffering should be set in the perspective of the Father's concern for his children's growth to maturity.

Now, maturity implies awareness of self, with its inclinations to good and to evil and its possibilities for free choice. It also involves knowledge of one's position in a society which gives and takes from everybody, and consciousness that such exchange must be an exchange of love because there is no other way to practise the precept of charity – not just at a material level, but also and chiefly for spiritual improvement. This is why Catherine strongly stresses the importance of association with one's neighbours:

> I want you to know that every virtue is practised by means of one's neighbours and likewise every fault. They who stay in hatred of me are harmful to their neighbours and to themselves, their nearest neighbours. (D, VI)

Once a soul has well established itself in charity it will be impelled to share its treasure with others:

> A soul in love with my truth never refrains from being of help to the whole world . . .
> Once one has improved oneself by the union of love he has made with me . . . he extends his desire to the salvation of the whole world . . . He helps his neighbours according to the various gifts I have given him to administer, either by teaching or sincerely advising, and by the example of a good, holy, honourable life. (D, VII)

God does appreciate the wish to atone for sin, but he does not want us to think that is all he expects from us. Sin cannot do him any harm, but it does harm sinners, the creatures he loves. So, rather than offering atonement for sin, our efforts should be aimed at preventing sin by co-operating with the Father in tutoring our fellow beings to fullness of life through knowledge of truth. This is, we may assume, what is meant by the likeness of the blessed Trinity impressed in our souls: it does not make us just a fine work of art to admire; it lends such energy as is needed to contribute to the welfare of the universe, and particularly to that of humankind, as we are required to do. Sharing of truth is the richest gift of charity. It is not so easy to practise as giving material help. It requires discernment and such self-denial as springs from genuine love. But it is what Christ did and wants us to do: 'First sweet Truth' said he had come that we might have life 'and have it to the full' (John 10:10), and showed us the way in the almost incredible conjoining of his own eternal bliss with the cruel suffering of his crucifixion. Our way of offering the charity of truth cannot differ from his own.

When still a child Catherine had been given to understand that truth is the most important of all goods to be shared with neighbours in obedience to the precept of charity. And she felt attracted to the Order of Preachers on learning that St Dominic wanted his friars to be givers of truth. The notion that striving for the salvation of our fellow-beings means patient bearing of all kinds of hardships makes a twin thread running all through the *Dialogue*. In answer to her petition for Raymond's welfare Catherine is told:

> Dear child, this is what I want him to seek: to please me, the Truth, in earnest hunger for the salvation of souls and great concern. But this, neither he nor anybody else could do without many persecutions . . . such as I will grant them. According to your wish to see my honour in holy Church, you shall conceive love for suffering with true patience, and this is how he and you and my other servants will prove that you do care for my honour. Then shall he be my darling child and find his rest on my only-begotten Son's breast. Of him I have made a bridge for you, to reach the goal of your life. (D, XX)

And when Catherine is told how important it is to go along the bridge and what it means, the twinning of apostolate and suffering is newly stressed:

> It is fitting for you all to go along this bridge, striving for the glory and praise of my name, painfully bearing many hardships, in the footsteps of the sweet loving Word: there is no other way for you to come to me. (D, XXIII)

To give glory to the Father by striving for the salvation of souls is how Catherine views the mission of the Word incarnate. This mission, she says, is what every Christian should try to make his own.

The *Dialogue* will develop at leisure the concept of the close connection between engagement in apostolate and suffering in the teaching about tears and in that on Divine Providence, but suffering is first dealt with from the perspective of its help to spiritual growth when Catherine is told how the soul rises from the first to the second step of the bridge, which means from imperfect, servile, self-centred love, to pure friendly love, untarnished by self-concern. The ascent is fostered by prayer which throws light on the knowledge of self and of God, but prayer itself is not void of danger because one might grow so attached to the pleasure to be found in it, as to forget that the aim of prayer should be to praise God, not to please the person who prays. Then God would help by withdrawing all comfort, and make one struggle against temptation:

> This I do that they may come to perfect knowledge of themselves and understand that they are nothing on their own account and no grace is theirs, so that in time of trial they have recourse to me, acknowledge that I am their benefactor, and seek nothing but me with true humility. This is why I give or draw back delight, not grace. (D, LX)

Aridity of mind, prayer becoming boring, make us realize that for all our efforts we cannot get rid of such troubles. But at the same time we are made conscious of our freedom, of our own ability not to consent to any suggestion that may be presented to the mind. In this twofold consciousness we shall find the strength to rise above ourselves, while faith in God's loving care will make us assured that we can overcome any obstacle on our way:

> God wants nothing but our welfare: he will not impose on us more than we can bear. Be comforted and do not try to avoid suffering; take care that your good will may have no rest except in [loving] what Christ loved and [hating] what God hated. And so, being armed with hatred and love, our will shall get such fortitude that, as St Paul says (Rom 8:35–39), neither the world nor the devil and the flesh, will make us leave this way. Let us endure, dearest brother, since the heavier load we carry in our lifetime with Christ crucified, the brighter glory shall we be given, and no suffering will be better rewarded than the pain of the heart and mental suffering because they are the hardest and are worth greater reward. (L, 225)

Painful mental struggle will have its first reward in the soul's increased strength and capacity to oppose its enemies:

Now, what would a soul be worth unless it bears many labours and temptations, from whatever side and in whichever way God may grant them? Its virtue would not have stood the test, since virtue is tested by its contrary. You can see that humility is acquired through pride: when one feels tempted by pride, on becoming aware of it he immediately turns to humility. Had he not been tempted, he would not have come to know himself as well. Once he has humbled himself on having come to see, he conceives such hatred [for pride] that he rejoices in any trial and injury he may have to bear. He behaves like a brave knight who does not avoid blows ... know, then, that we should not flee away or complain in time of darkness because light shines out of darkness. (L, 211)

God is a good trainer and wants his children to grow to full maturity. He wants them not to remain with delight in sweet milk, but to enjoy hard bread, even should their gums bleed; not to waste time in children's games but bravely to fight so that truth may prevail.[1]

The positive outcome of our struggling against temptation resulting in additional strength of mind is a favourite topic with Catherine.

You are staying on the battlefield of this darksome life in restless struggle against your enemies ... Our enemies are never asleep; they are ever on the alert [for openings] to cause us trouble. God allows them to do so to afford us everyday opportunities to acquire merit and rise from the sleep of sloth. You know that, when one is made aware that enemies are assailing, he makes no delay in opposing them because he understands that, should he be asleep, he risks being killed. God makes us aware of them, that we may wake up and take hold of the weapon, hatred and love. Hatred shuts vice out of the door of consent by opposing unbending displeasure, and opens it to virtue, stretching out the arms of love to welcome it to the soul with great desire.

You see, then, that it is good indeed that enemies should rise against us. We must not, and cannot, be afraid, provided we make use of our free will; we must find comfort in saying: 'With the help of Christ crucified we can do anything.' (L, 257)

To win our battle we have to follow his example:

Our king behaves as a true knight who insists in fighting until his enemies are defeated ... by his wisdom he overcame the malicious cunning of the devil. In fact, with his bare hands nailed to the cross, he overthrew the prince of this world. (L, 256)

Christ had no need of any weapon, except his own divine all-powerful love, and the same weapon must be ours: if we want to win our own combat, we have to imitate him.

> We should provide ourselves with the weapon of fortitude joined to most ardent charity, since it is for the sake of supreme eternal Goodness that we must be willing to bear any pain and labour. Such weapon is so delightful and strong that neither the devil's manifold temptations nor mockery and injury from human beings can deprive the soul of the fortitude and delight it enjoys when staying in sweet charity.

When so armed, a soul will rather deal blows to the devil than be hurt by his assaults: the enemy will be defeated on realizing that, far from being scared by temptation, the soul gladly welcomes trouble for the sake of Christ crucified.

> We cannot avoid fighting, while staying in our mortal body, . . . in different ways, as it pleases God's kindness to grant. If one was not armed, he would be wounded by impatience, and by pleasure in consenting . . . and would be killed by his staying in mortal sin. (L, 169)

Every human being can use this strong weapon – patient fortitude, the offspring of knowledge and love – it is within reach and nobody can prevent us from using it. Such assurance can make us bold and cheerful in the very midst of the struggle:

> We must not try to avoid blows, and must enjoy staying on the battlefield as long as we live. Nobody who comes to be aware of the fruit of fighting, could avoid wishing for it with great desire. No victory without fighting, and lack of victory means blame. (Ibid.)

A brave knight, being efficiently armed with patience and love, will not go in search of 'dubious fields' on which to fight his battle: he will not make his own choice of trials in the vain hope to have done with struggling once for all; he will not, because he enjoys fighting and knows that there is no other way to glory.[2]

Having thus mastered the natural fear of pain, which is the hallmark of imperfect love, the soul rises to the second step of the bridge and is introduced into 'the cave' of Christ's breast, there to get an opening to 'the secret of the heart': the divine love that stands at the root of his passion. Here the soul's disposition to suffering comes to a decisive turn: fear gives way to desire, a desire to conform to the Lord's own sufferings, because awareness of his boundless love overcomes self-concern; the timid, imperfect, servile love of the first stage has become friendly love, its object is now 'the friend', not any advantage that might come from friendship. Friendly love is perfect love, and will soon grow to the utmost perfection of filial love: the love of the Word incarnate for his heavenly Father. At this level the soul will be so united to Christ as to feel involved in his own mission, that of giving glory to the Father by working for the welfare of neighbours in such perfect union as gives it a share in the power of the Father, the Wisdom of the Son, and the love of the Holy Spirit:

> I granted him to share in his will the charity which is the Holy Spirit, by fortifying his will in the desire to bear hardships, and go out for my name's sake, and give birth to virtues in [dealing with] his neighbours. (D, LXXIV)

This does not mean going out of the house of self-knowledge, but letting the virtues conceived in love go abroad according to the needs of our neighbours, which can easily be done once the fear of losing our consolation is overcome and we have stopped worrying about ourselves.

This is what the apostles did after receiving the Holy Spirit; this is what caused St Paul to say that his boast was in "insults, hardships, persecutions" (cf. 2 Cor 12:9–10). When a soul has been so deeply impressed with the wounds of the Crucified that its will has been made one with the will of Christ, then fear turns to desire of suffering and painful patience to delight:

> To such most beloved children pain is delight and delight is labour, and such is any occasional worldly comfort and pleasure . . . they even spurn any mental consolation they may be given by me, the eternal Father: they despise it out of humility and hatred of self. Not that they spurn the consolation and the gift of my grace, they spurn the delight that the soul's desire finds in such consolation. (D, LXXVIII)

God is ever present in these very perfect creatures: he has his rest in their souls, so that whenever, under the pressure of loving desire, they may be seeking for him, they can sense his presence. To them 'every place is the right place, and every time the right time for prayer'. Having risen above earthly concerns to the height of heaven by the ladder of virtues, they have found rest and food in the blessed Trinity: the food of Christ's presence in the Eucharist, the food of the souls to be saved in the way of his doctrine, with the ministry of the Holy Spirit:

> Such are the followers of the immaculate Lamb, my only-begotten Son. While staying on the cross he was blissful and in pain; he was in pain in bearing his bodily sufferings together with the cross of his desire to atone for the faults of mankind, and blissful because the Godhead united to his human nature could not suffer and in its unveiled sight his soul was filled with bliss. (Ibid.)

This bewildering experience – the coexistence of delight and pain in one individual at one time – can be attributed to the simultaneous presence, in the person of Christ, of the divine nature and the human. It is more surprising in normal human beings, though not impossible, and might even appear natural if we remember that increase in love causes increase in suffering, as Catherine states, no doubt from her own experience. Besides, patient suffering is an unfailing witness to the presence of love in the soul, the tree of love whose marrow is patience. To make his love known to humankind and to kindle love in the hearts of men and women, the heavenly Father imposed on his own Son the awful sufferings of the crucifixion, and made the cross the chair for his teaching. If we grasp the meaning of it all, pleasure will taste bitter and bitterness will prove sweet, so that, could we acquire virtues and eternal life without suffering, we would refuse to go along the plain, pleasant way, and choose the hard one, that of the valiant who enjoy picking roses out of thorns, for the sake not of the thorns, but of the King whose crown is made of thorns.

The teaching on the gradual ascent of the soul to perfect love through suffering (or, we might say, the mutual increase of love and pain) so pleases Catherine, and her sorrow for the ignorance of those who misunderstand the value of trials so spurs her desire, that she is eager for further instruction. Having understood that there is no progress without pain, she asks First Truth to tell her all about tears:

> the variety of tears, and how they were produced, and whence they came, and how many kinds of tears there were. (D, LXXXVII)

The answer covers a rather large section of the *Dialogue*. Catherine is first told that tears are of five different kinds, and that not all are good: some foster life, and others cause death. Their quality depends on the disposition of the person who sheds them.

> I want you to understand that all tears proceed from the heart since no organ in the body is so ready to respond to the heart as the eye. If the heart aches the eye makes it known, and if the pain is sensual it weeps cordial tears breeding death, because they proceed from a heart whose love is unruly, not in tune with me. And its being disordered offends me and is given deadly sorrow and tears. (D, LXXXVIII)

'Deadly tears' are wept by the wicked who stay in the swollen river under the bridge and do not care about the bridge's safe way: they prefer staying where they are, and drip their tears into the swiftly flowing waters. Having no hold, they are irresistibly drawn by the current and glide to the dead waters of damnation. Their misunderstanding of the value of suffering and refusal of trials with excessive sensitivity to personal mishaps and no concern for neighbours make them weep: their tears are the output of hearts that are dead because they ignore true love, which is life to the soul. Still it is not impossible that sense of deadly danger may waken the will to its responsibility and cause the soul to make its way out of the river. Then tears turn from deadly to life-giving ones in a gradual progress towards perfection strictly bound to the progress in love.

Vital tears in their first stage are a mixture of love and fear. Their initial motion is fear of helpless ruin advising trying to go ashore. Once out of the river, the soul will turn its attention to the bridge and to those who are going on it in spite of the big river flowing beneath their feet. Fear gave the start, but now love begins to draw to the bridge, Christ crucified, almost compelling a return of love by the disclosure of his own love. But his sacrifice may require most generous answers, which will make a beginner perplexed: how far will love pretend to lead him? Trials, in fact, will not fail to come and offer good opportunities for the soul to fight its way and improve its strength. Self-concern will still weigh on it, but it will be of a spiritual kind: fear of missing eternal bliss in the vision of Godhead including, perhaps unconsciously, faith and love.

> See, now, the tears that begin to give life: the tears of those who, on becoming aware of their faults, are caused to weep for fear of

chastisement. Such tears are heartfelt and sensual, which means that, though they have not attained perfect hatred of their sins because of the offence to me, they rise with heartfelt sorrow for the chastisement that follows upon sin, and the eye weeps because it has to comply with the pain of the heart.

Then, through the practice of virtues, the soul begins to lose fear, as it comes to realize that fear alone is not sufficient, by itself, to earn eternal life ... Then love makes it rise to knowledge of self and of my kindness to it, and it begins to hope in my mercy, in which [hope] the heart rejoices, sorrow for sin being mingled with hope of my divine mercy. The eye, then, starts weeping tears that spring from the fountain of the heart. (D, LXXXIX)

At this stage tears are still far from being perfect, because they are rooted in a spiritual kind of love eager for consolation and ready to avoid trials. Attachment to one's will has not been overcome yet, so that in time of temptation or persecution

the eye, on sensing the suffering of the heart, starts weeping tender, self-compassionate tears, springing from spiritual love of self.

Then, by staying in the twofold light of knowledge, the soul will conceive displeasure for its own faults, and a 'fire of love' for God's kindness. Love of God opens the heart to love of neighbours and makes it proof against the appeals of self: love overcomes fear. This decisive turning takes place on the second step of the bridge, where the soul is shown 'the secret of the heart', God's boundless love causing Christ to die on the cross to rescue mankind from death. Fear being lost, one's will freely unites to God's will. The soul, at this point,

begins to have joy and compassion; it rejoices in love and is filled with compassion for neighbours ... Then the eye, that wants to comply with the heart's desire, weeps in charity for me and neighbours, with cordial love, and no concern except for my having been offended and for the injury to fellow-beings, not for any personal harm ... he is unmindful of himself and his only concern is to give glory and honour to my name; with struggling desire he delights to take his food on the table of the most holy cross, and conform to the humble, patient, immaculate Lamb. (Ibid.)

This is what happens on the third step, where love turns from friendly to filial, as the soul receives from Christ the kiss of peace sealing the union. Tears that spring from most perfect love are marked by the same, utmost perfection. Struggle against fear and self-concern is now over: hardships are no longer feared, they are desired and it is no longer a matter of patient enduring: they are sought as means for a closer union with Christ:

> Having so pleasantly gone along the bridge by following the doctrine of my sweet Truth in bearing with true sweet patience any pain or trouble I granted for its salvation, [the soul] has met them bravely, not after its own choice, but according to mine. It does not stop at patient acceptance: it bears them cheerfully. To be persecuted for my name is its glory, whatever it may have to suffer, and the soul comes to such delight and peace as no tongue can tell. . . .
>
> Then it has its rest in me, the peaceful sea. The heart is united to me under the impulse of love, as I told you it was in the fourth, the unitive state. In sensing the presence of my eternal Godhead the eye begins to shed sweet tears which, like genuine milk, nourish the soul in true patience. They are a sweetly scented ointment, pleasant to smell. . . .
>
> This is the supreme stage, where the soul is blissful and sorrowful. Blissful it is because of its union with me where it has a taste of divine love, and afflicted by the sight of the offences to my goodness and greatness. . . .
>
> The unitive state, breeding tears of great sweetness, is not hindered by the knowledge of self within the charity for neighbours, where it found tears of love for my divine mercy and sorrow for the offences of neighbours, so that it wept with those who mourn and rejoiced with those who rejoice (cf. Rom 12:15). Such are those who live in charity, and at them the soul rejoices. (Ibid.)

At the top of its progress love reaches the plenitude of its dynamism; then it has to go out and expand, attain full perfection by loving God in neighbours, as in the love of God it finds cause for loving neighbours, and in them it is afforded the means to practise love of God, which is, as Catherine says, 'to walk with both feet'. When a soul has grown so high in holy desire, it simply cannot wish for anything except God's will. Love makes it weep in sorrow for offences to God and damage to people. Still, the devil is not asleep – we, the lazy sleepers, have something to learn from him –

but he cannot do any harm to a soul who is all afire with love, because the warmth of charity and the perfume of union with God are too much for him. Whenever he tries to approach such a soul:

> he flees away as does a fly from a boiling pot, being scared by its warmth. Were it lukewarm he would not be afraid; he would get in, though sometimes he might perish in it on finding it warmer than he expected. (D, XC)

This rather ridiculous situation sounds like a reflection of Catherine's own experience, when devils invaded her cell 'like most annoying swarms of flies' trying to dissuade her from ascetic practices but had to yield to her constancy relying on God's help.[3]

In a soul all afire with love, 'tears of the eye' give way to 'tears of fire':

> I still have to tell you, and satisfy the desire you expressed, about some who long for perfect tears and feel unable to obtain them: is there any other way of weeping than by tears of the eye? Yes, there is a weeping of fire, of true holy desire, burning out itself under the pressure of love: one would gladly consume his life in displeasure of self and for the salvation of souls, but feels unable to.
>
> I tell you that their tears are tears of fire in which the Holy Spirit weeps before me for them and for their neighbours, as my divine charity kindles by its own flame the soul that offers earnest longing without weeping. I tell you that such tears are made of fire, and this is why I said that the Holy Spirit weeps. On feeling unable to weep, they offer their desires of weeping for love of me. Though, should they open their mind's eye, they would see that whenever one of my servants offers the perfume of holy desire and humble, continuous prayer, the Holy Spirit is weeping through him. (D, XCI)

The action of the Holy Spirit responding to the soul's desire, as figured in the fire from heaven burning up Elijah's sacrifice, has now come to its fulfilment and one might think that, no further tutoring being needed, one might spend the time given in peaceful union with God. But it is not so. In fact, opportunities for further ascent are ever open, as are opportunities to go back and lose what one has got. We, the sleepy beings, are standing between two rivals: on one side the evil spirit ever on the alert for the chance to make us fall and, on the other, God, never losing sight of the darling child in his care. He knows that no human being, however perfect, is proof against the enticement of an easier life, and that consciousness of his victory over the many obstacles he found on his way might breed pride, the root of all sins. To prevent any misgivings, God makes use of a double sort of tactics: while insisting on his radical pruning to urge him on, he allows his pupil to fail to make the right choice in slight matters, just to remind him that he is not quite proof against temptation and should still be on the alert:

> Sometimes I make use of a pleasant trick to keep them in the virtue of humility: I will permit their sensuality to fall asleep so that, just as happens when one is asleep, they feel as if they had no feelings, no will . . . I say that they feel as if their sensuality were asleep: they can bear heavy burdens without being conscious of their weight. Then because of a trifle, a little incident amounting to nothing such as may cause one, afterwards, to make fun of himself, his own trouble will make him amazed. This is my providence's doing to make him grow and go down to the valley of humility. (D, CXLV)

The other aspect of God's tactics is to insist on radical pruning. He does as the vinedresser in the parable of the vine and its branches (John 15:2): he prunes them sensibly to make them yield more and better fruit:

> Every single event do I permit within my providence: life and death, in whatever way, hunger and thirst, loss of worldly status, nakedness, cold and warmth, insults, mockery, villainous words. Such things I permit to be said or done. . . .
>
> Sometimes I may let the whole world stand against an honourable man, and allow him to end his life in such a way as will cause worldly people greatly to wonder. They will judge it unfair to see such a man die either in water or in fire, or being throttled by wild beasts, or losing his bodily life under the ruins of his own house. How unbecoming such events appear to an eye that is not enlightened by faith! But not so to a believer, because he has found out, on being urged by love, how to savour my providence in the great things I mentioned [creation and redemption] and this is why he sees and believes that whatever I do, is done according to my providence, and to no other aim than the salvation of souls. (D, CXXXVII)

To evidence the mysterious ways of divine Providence, Catherine is reminded of a 'particular event' – the object of her fourth petition – that of the young man sentenced to death, first rebelling against the cruelty of his doom, then coming to see his execution as the wedding feast of his soul coming to enjoy its endless blissful union to Godhead.

> Do you want me, child, to tell you how the world is deceived when trying to penetrate my mysteries? Open your mind's eye and look into me, and by gazing you will come to see [it is so] in the particular event of which I promised I would tell you . . .
>
> I want you to understand that to spare him eternal damnation in which, as you see, he was, I permitted this event so that by his own blood he might have life, in the blood of Truth, my only-begotten Son. (D, CXXXIX)

To exchange mortal life for life everlasting is no doubt a good bargain, but to admit it is, one must be enlightened by faith.

That God's educational proceedings to free from sin and lead us to perfection are aimed at making us able to spread the good seed of truth is clearly stated when the teaching on divine providence comes to its conclusion:

> Now I have told you, and you have perceived, not so much as the scent of a sprinkle which is really nothing if compared to the sea, how I provide for my creatures, in general and in particular . . . I once told you, as you can remember, that by the means of my servants I would be merciful to the world, and reform my bride through much suffering. (D, CXLVI)

In fact, once a soul has climbed the three steps by gradually perfecting its way to love, it becomes so closely united to Christ crucified that it cannot avoid sharing his mission. Hunger for souls to be saved then grows so strong that suffering turns to pleasure because that is the way to help them to salvation in close union with the Saviour.

> Being in love with my love and eager for the food they relish, souls to be saved, they rush to the table of the most holy cross, because they want to be of help to their neighbours through pain and much suffering. (D, LXXVIII)

Suffering lovingly borne makes them happy because it is the hallmark of union with Christ crucified.

> They truly can be said to be another Christ, my only-begotten Son, because they have undertaken to share his task. He came as peace-maker, to put a stop to war and reconcile man to me in

peace by his great suffering unto the shameful death on the cross, and they too go about in the sign of the cross and are made peace-makers by means of prayer and speech and the example they give of a good and holy life. Their virtues shine like gems in their patiently bearing offences. Such are their hooks in fishing for souls. (D, CXLVII)

Fishing with a hook must have seemed too slow to Catherine; her desire flies all over the boundless sea, wanting to catch all the fish in it. To learn the rules for fruitful fishing, she focuses on two remarkable catches recorded in the Gospel, one during the Lord's lifetime (Luke 5:4–8) and the other after his resurrection (John 21:1–8). The net, she notes, has to be dropped from starboard, the right side of true love, not from that of selfish interest, and not in the night of sinful life, but in day-time when the soul is alight with the sun of divine grace. The fishermen should be humble enough to call for help from the men in other boats, when they realize that the catch is too heavy for them to draw ashore. They should, above all, keep in mind that success is due to faith, the faith that moved Peter to obey the man on the shore in spite of his own unsuccessful efforts all night long.

All the events in the life of Christ, Catherine notes, include a teaching for us to understand, a guiding line to follow. He in fact first did what he would in due time preach.

> This have I told you to make you understand how providentially my Truth behaved during his stay with you . . . and what the soul does when it has risen to such perfect level. Mind that one does so more perfectly than another depending on his promptness to obey the word and on his enjoying more perfect light by having lost self-reliance and completely relying on me his Creator. . . . The perfection of their catching is proportional to the perfection of their dropping [the net]. (D, CXLVII)

In fishing for souls the success of a fisherman depends on the perfect harmony in the powers of his soul, showing that the disorder sin had sown among them has been overcome.[4]

> All their senses make a sweetest sound coming forth from the city of the soul, because all its doors are shut and open. Will is shut to love of self and open to desire and love of my honour and benevolence to neighbours. Intellect is closed to the sight of worldly pleasures and vanities and miseries, all of which are black night darkening the mind that indulges in looking at them, and it

is open in the light having for its object the light of my Truth. Memory is locked to the remembrance of the world and of its own sensuality and is wide open to receive and keep the remembrance of my gifts. The affective bent of the soul then makes such a joyful melody, its strings being tuned with prudence and skill to the same note: glory and praise of my name. (D, CXLVII)

Bodily senses too are tuned to the same note so that they all do what they are meant to do: they respond to the soul as the pipes of an organ do to the touch of the organist on the keyboard. There is a pleasure in dealing with people who have established such lovely harmony in soul and body that not even the wicked can fail to appreciate

and quite a number are caught by this hook and instrument, so that they part from death and come to life.

All saints have fished by means of this organ. The first who made it sound life was the sweet loving Word on assuming your human nature. By humanity united to Godhead he made such a sweet sound on the cross that he caught humankind, the [missing] child. He also caught the devil and deprived him of the long-lasting lordship he had had because of sin. (Ibid.)[5]

All of you learn how to play [your organ] from this teacher. Having learnt from him, the apostles started sowing his word all over the world. Martyrs and confessors, doctors and virgins, all caught souls by their melodies. Look at Ursula, the glorious virgin: so sweetly did she play her instrument that she caught eleven thousand virgins, and more than as many persons did she catch by the same sound. Likewise all the others in various ways. Who caused them? My boundless providence supplying the instruments, and the way and the means to play them. Whatever I grant them or permit is meant to perfect their instruments, provided they are willing to understand. (Ibid.)

The action of divine Providence, its caring at the same time for the welfare of the universe and the needs of every single creature and, besides, God's kindness in asking his little creatures to have a share in his own work is truly amazing, and Catherine is at a loss about how to respond. The voice speaking to her seems to echo her feelings:

Let your heart grow wider, dear child, and open the eye of your mind in the light of faith to see how lovingly and providently I created man and disposed him so that he may come to enjoy my supreme eternal goodness. I have provided for everything, as I told you, for soul and body, in the imperfect and the perfect, in heaven and on earth, during mortal life and for life immortal. (D, CXLVIII)

Catherine's God is, without doubt, 'God not of the dead but of the living' (Matt 22:32): he sent his Son to us that we may 'have life, and life abundant' (John 8:32). The opportunities for fullness of life that he offers we can either accept to our advantage or refuse to our harm.

The complex action of divine Providence as seen by Catherine appears, then, aimed at leading man to fullness of life through perfection of love. This is why her teaching on Providence is immediately followed by the teaching on *obedience*.

Obedience is the test of true love. Christ said to his disciples: 'If you love me you will keep my commandments' (John 14:15). It is the means we are given to practise love. But obedience cannot be said to be a popular virtue: it is considered as an obstacle to human freedom, a 'passive virtue', in spite of the contradiction in the terms. With Catherine it is a true virtue, in the full meaning of the word, one to be acquired by the soul by voluntary, generous exertion. It is the conscious answer to the requirements of the truth about God and man, implying a right understanding of the relationship between Godhead and humanity.

On introducing this subject, the Word incarnate, whose mission St Paul summed up in his being obedient to the Father unto death on the cross (Phil 2:8), is presented as the model for us to copy. But Catherine has to find out the key to his obedience:

What caused the Word to be so obedient? His love for my honour and the salvation of souls. Where did love come from? From his soul's clear vision of the divine Essence and eternal Trinity, since it ever saw me, God eternal.

But we, still on our way, do not enjoy a direct vision of Godhead and must find a substitute for it in the light of faith:

Such vision perfectly caused [in him] that fidelity which the light of most holy faith imperfectly effects in you. He in fact was loyal to me, his eternal Father, and therefore he hurried in that glorious light, like one in love, along the way of obedience. (D, CLIV)

Light of faith widening the range of the light of reason gifts the soul with discernment, the distinctive virtue of the rational creature, and points out in Christ's example the way for us to go. In the same light man comes to a right understanding of himself. It shows that what God requires of him is to conform to the law of his nature, the law of love that he gave to it and that is for ever its own law. To obey God is fully to be oneself at one's best. Whatever he created was meant to foster life and what he requires is not difficult to do,

> it is easy, since nothing is so easy and pleasant as love, and what I require of you is nothing but to love and cherish me and your neighbours. This can be done at any time, in any place or position one may be, by loving and keeping everything for the praise and honour of my name. (D, LV)

Love is an arch spanning the history of mankind as well as the story of every man and woman; obedience and patience help to build it:

> Fall in love, dearest child, with this glorious virtue. Do you want to prove grateful for the gifts you have been given by me, the eternal Father? Be obedient, and obedience will show your gratitude, because it proceeds from love. It shows that you are not ignorant, because it comes from knowledge of my Truth and is, therefore, a good acquired in the knowledge of the Word, who opened to you, as your rule, the way of obedience by making himself obedient unto the shameful death on the cross. (D, CLXIII)

Christ's obedience is the key that opens the door of heaven; it simply opens the door, but stays outside while charity in its wedding robe enters. And charity is the measure for the merit of obedience:

> Were you to ask: whose merit is greater ... ? I tell you that the merit of obedience does not stand in the action, or in the place, or in the person who obeys, whether lay or religious, but according to the measure of love in obeying. (D, CLXIV)

God's justice requires it should be so, because all human beings, whatever each one's condition in life, must be offered the way to perfection:

> Merit, as I already told you and say again, is acknowledged according to the truly obedient's measure of love so that

149

everybody, in whatever condition, may perfectly acquire merit which I placed in nothing but love.

Some I call to one status, some to another, according to each one's capacities, but everyone has his fill according to the measure of his love, as I already said. If a secular's love is greater than that of a religious he shall be accorded more [merit], and likewise a religious [will gain greater merit if he loves] better than a lay person. And so with all the others. (Ibid.)

All of you have I placed in the vineyard of obedience to work in different ways. Each one will be given his reward according to the measure of love, not according to the work done or the time employed . . . Some are put to work in this vineyard in their childhood; some come later, some in old age, but will get so afire with love on realizing the short limits of their time, that they will catch up those who came in early age and have been going on at leisure. From its love of obedience, then, does each soul earn merit and fill itself with me, the peaceful sea. (D, CLXV)

War is over, peace is restored. Peace between God and man, in the union of will; peace in the powers of the human soul, newly bound by love to harmonious collaboration; peace with the universe once man has stopped rebelling against God and sealed love's covenant.[6]

Peace is the inward reward of the obedient: his very life 'shouts out peace', and death will disclose to his soul the 'vision of peace', and fill it to the brim in the ocean of God's goodness and love.

Notes

1. Cf. L, 333.
2. Cf. L, 201.
3. Cf. *Life*, 108.
4. Cf. D, XXI: 'Sin sprouted thorns and thistles with many troubles, the creature found rebellion in itself, no sooner man rebelled against me than he rebelled against himself.'
5. In early Christian iconography the image of Orpheus calming wild animals and drawing them to him is sometimes substituted for that of the Good Shepherd as a symbol of Christ. It can be seen in some Roman catacombs, but Catherine had finished dictating the *Dialogue* before her stay in Rome and the image must have come to her through other channels.
6. The end of nature's rebellion against man is seen by Catherine in the 'miracles of obedience' by water, fire, earth and air, the four elements constituting the universe, according to current notions: cf. D, CLXV.

Postscript

Stay in the cell of self-knowledge
there to keep and spend
the treasure I have given you:
a doctrine of truth founded on the rock,
Christ the sweet Jesus. (D, CLXVI)

Should we try to summarize the precious treasure of the doctrine entrusted to Catherine for her own and everybody's improvement we might find that it can be summed up in two words: knowledge and love. Knowledge that leads to love, and love seeking in knowledge the object it is need of. And, if we were to look for the source of this doctrine, we would have to go back to the primary teaching that the Lord imparted to Catherine when she began to venture in the mysterious land of the spirit:

You are she who is not, and I am He Who Am. (*Life*, 92)

Such a radical exclusion of any possibility for man of finding in himself a cause for his own existence, when confronted with actual existence finds a reasonable answer in creation as a gratuitous act of love. This is an answer that cannot stay at the level of a concept with no impact on sentiment; it kindles love since 'it is the condition of love that, as soon as one sees oneself loved, one starts loving' (L, 29). This is a basic concept staying within the range of reason: 'it is simply reasonable that having come to know you, one should love you' (P, I).

Faith throws further light on it: the sacrifice of the Word incarnate draws us into the chasm of God's love: knowledge of love as supreme truth shines bright from the height of the cross and draws man's heart from step to step to its highest perfection – to union with God: 'Those who are clad in the vestment of charity . . . are another myself because their will is made one with mine' (D, I).

This is the treasure entrusted to Catherine to keep and share with all of us. Her gratitude for the gift bursts forth in the warm hymn of thankful praise concluding her *Dialogue*, where the interaction of love and knowledge is most effectively depicted in the mirror held by love's hand:

Thanks, thanks to you, eternal Father, who have not despised me, your own work, nor turned your face from me, nor spurned my desires. You, light, have not considered my darkness; you, life, have not withdrawn from me, who am death, nor you, the physician, because of my severe illness; you, eternal purity, [have not avoided] my being full of mud and miseries; you, the Infinite, my finiteness; you, wisdom, my foolishness.

Because of these, and of many more endless evils and faults in me, your wisdom, your goodness, your kind disposition and your endless goodness have not spurned me, but by your light you have given me light. In your wisdom I have come to know the truth, in your clemency have I found your charity, and love of my neighbour. Who compelled you? No virtue of mine: nothing but your own charity.

Let the same love compel you to enlighten my mind's eye with the light of faith, that I may know the truth you open to me. Grant that my memory may keep [the remembrance of] your gifts, and that it will be set afire with your charity, and that such fire may make my body flourish and bleed, so that with the same blood, given for the sake of [Christ's] blood, and with the key of obedience, I may unlock the gate of heaven.

The same I heartily ask you for all rational creatures, for all and each of them, and for the mystical body of holy Church. I confess, and do not deny, that you loved me before I existed, and that you love me ineffably, as if foolishly in love with your creature.

O Trinity eternal, O Godhead! Your divine nature gave value to the price, the blood of your Son. You, eternal Trinity, are a profound sea, so that the more I enter it the more I find, and the more I find the more I seek for you. You do not satiate, because the soul that feeds at its pleasure in your depth does not feel satiated: it always remains hungry for you, thirsty for you, eternal

Trinity, because it longs to see you in your own light. As a hart desires the spring of living water, so does my soul wish to get out of its prison, this dark body, and see you in truth. How long will your face be hidden to my sight?

O eternal Trinity, fire and depth of charity! Dissolve this cloud, my body. The knowledge of you that you have given me in your truth compels me to desire that I may leave my heavy body and give my life for the glory and praise of your name because I have tasted and seen by the light of understanding, in your own light, your depths, eternal Trinity, and the beauty of your creature. Looking at myself in you, I saw me as your own image, since you gifted me from your own power, eternal Father, and from your wisdom in my understanding, which wisdom is appropriated to your only-begotten Son; the Holy Spirit proceeding from you and from your Son has given me will that I may love.

You, eternal Father, are the maker, and I, your creature, have come to know, in your creating me anew by the blood of your Son, that you are in love with the beauty of your work.

O depth, O eternal Godhead, O sea profound! How could you have given me more than to give me yourself? You are a fire ever burning without consuming; you are a fire whose warmth burns away from the soul all selfishness; you are a fire removing cold; you shed light . . . Truly, this light is a sea; because it feeds the soul with you, the peaceful sea. In your light you have made me know your truth: you are that supreme light lending supernatural light to the mind's eye, so abundantly and perfectly that you make the light of faith brighter. In that faith I see that my soul is alive, and in this light it receives you, light.

In the light of faith I acquire wisdom in the wisdom of the Word, your Son; in the light of faith I am strong, constant and persevering; in the light of faith I hope: it does not allow me to fail on my way. This light shows me the way: without it I should walk in darkness, and this is why I begged you, eternal Father, to enlighten me with the light of most holy faith.

This light is indeed a sea, because it feeds the soul with you, the peaceful sea, eternal Trinity. Its water is not troubled and therefore the soul has no fear because it knows the truth; it is so clear that it lets hidden realities be seen, so that where the powerful light of your faith abounds, the soul is almost made certain of what it believes. It is a mirror, reflecting what you, eternal Trinity, let me know because, as I look into this mirror, holding it with the hand of love, it makes me see me, your creature, in you, and you in me by the union that you made of your divinity with our humanity.

This light makes me know; it shows me you, supreme and infinite Good: good above any good, blissful, incomprehensible, inestimable Good. Beauty above any beauty, wisdom above all wisdom: you are Wisdom itself. You, the food of angels, all afire with love, have given yourself to men. You, the vestment clothing our nakedness, feed the hungry with your sweetness. You are sweet, and no bitterness in you.

O Trinity eternal, in your light, which you lent me and I received by the light of most holy faith, through much admirable explaining, I have come to know the way to great perfection, so that I may serve you in light, not in darkness, and be a mirror of good and saintly life and rise from my miserable life, since by my own fault I have always been serving you in darkness. I have not come to know your truth, and therefore have not loved it. Why did I not know you? Because I did not see you in the glorious light of most holy faith, the cloud of self-love having darkened the eye of my understanding. And you, eternal Trinity, dissolved my darkness by your light.

Who can attain to your height and give you thanks for such a boundless gift and the great privilege I was given with your doctrine on truth? This is a particular grace above the general grace you grant to all your creatures. You kindly consented to comply with my need, and with that of the other creatures that will see themselves reflected in it.

Respond, Lord. It is you who gave, and you yourself must respond and satisfy by infusing in me the light of grace, so that by the same light I may return thanks to you.

Clothe me, clothe me with you, eternal Trinity, so that I may hasten along this mortal life with true obedience and in the light of most holy faith, which seems to be intoxicating my soul anew. Thanks to God. Amen. (D, CLXVII)

Yes, we can join Catherine in thanking God for the sound and comforting doctrine of truth that is love, of love that is God's and our own truth. And we should also be grateful to her for allowing the doctrine to penetrate her very life, so that in sharing it with us she is in no way a teacher imparting cold, abstract notions. Her mind and soul have been so moulded by the doctrine as to make them one with it, and her words are made a living flame shedding light and warmth.

Thank you, Catherine!

Index